MEMORY MAN

A Memoir

MEMORY MAN

A Memoir

JIMMY MAGEE ～

WITH JASON O'TOOLE

Gill & Macmillan

Gill & Macmillan
Hume Avenue, Park West, Dublin 12
with associated companies throughout the world
www.gillmacmillanbooks.ie

© Jimmy Magee 2012
978 07171 5352 7

Index compiled by Cover to Cover
Typography design by Make Communication
Print origination by O'K Graphic Design, Dublin
Printed and bound by Scandbook, Falun, Sweden 2012

This book is typeset in 13.5/17 pt Minion.

The paper used in this book comes from the wood pulp
of managed forests. For every tree felled, at least one tree
is planted, thereby renewing natural resources.

A CIP catalogue record for this book is available from the
British Library.

5 4 3 2

Dedicated to the lasting memory of
Marie and Paul
and to those they left behind
Linda, June, Patricia and Mark

CONTENTS

ACKNOWLEDGEMENTS

Thanks to Assumpta and Kevin O'Brien and family for kindness and understanding, particularly in difficult times.

To Mary Rose and Pat McParland for a lifetime of friendship.

To all at RTE and the *Sunday World*.

To members of the All-Stars for more than forty years of devotion and loyalty.

To Eimear O'Mahony for the caring job on TV's 'Different Class'.

To Doctors O'Rourke and Quigley and my great friend Father Brian D'Arcy, caring for me, body and soul.

To Ciara Drennan who transcribed the tapes.

To Jason O'Toole who understood it all.

| EARLY YEARS

I was a twelve-year-old boy listening on the wireless to the 1947 all-Ireland final between Kerry and Cavan in New York—the only one ever to be played outside Ireland—when I first dreamt about becoming a sports commentator. All these years later I still have to pinch myself when I reflect on how I have travelled more than a million miles and visited more than eighty-five countries in my broadcasting career, which is still going strong after six decades. It makes me, according to those who know these things, one of the longest-serving sports commentators in the world today.

For the first three thousand miles of those epic journeys I didn't have to pay the fare, nor did I select the journey or the mode of transport, because my mother brought me from my birthplace of New York to live in Ireland when I was three years old.

Even though both my parents were from north Co. Louth, they didn't know each other until they met in the Big Apple and fell head over in heels in love—as did thousands of other Irish expatriates who had left the old sod to seek their fortune. I'm not too sure how my father, Patrick Magee, met my mother, Rose Mackin, but if I was a betting man I'd put my money on them first clapping eyes on each other at a dance or at one of the frequent functions organised for Louth natives.

I was born on 31 January 1935 in the Bronx. I was the first-born of four children—two boys, myself and Seán, and two girls, Mary and Patricia—but, tragically, my younger brother, Seán, died as an infant. I have vivid memories of Seán, and even though I was too young to realise what was happening, I remember sensing that something was not right, as Seán was always ill and cried a lot. I don't know what the cause of death was, and strangely I have little recall of the death itself, but I do know that it was a devastating experience for my parents, and I doubt that they ever got fully over it.

At the time the threat of America entering the war was looming, and my parents, who were homesick anyway and were being drawn home, like everyone else, used this as an excuse to permanently move back to Ireland. I never spoke to them about it, but I believe their rationale was that America probably wasn't a place for young James to be growing up in.

It's something I can sympathise with, because many years later I got an offer of a job in Akron, Ohio, as a sports broadcaster and DJ. It would have been a perfect gig—the money and job package offered were very attractive—but I had two children at the time and I thought they would be better off being reared in Ireland than in America. To her credit, my wife, Marie, did encourage me to take the American job, because she could see I was really tempted, but I reluctantly turned down the offer and have never had any regrets or thought about the path my career might have taken. What's the point in having regrets? Life is too short for that.

To this day my ties with America are strong. I have an American passport as well as my Irish one, and I still get excited when I return to my birthplace. There's a buzz about the place that you get as soon as you leave JFK Airport and head towards the bright lights and the big city on the Long Island

Expressway, the excitement building as you pass Shea Stadium and then the magnificent skyline of Manhattan suddenly appears. Without fail, it always awakes special feelings in me; I don't know if that comes from the fact that I was born there.

Travel has become a very important part of my life. It's funny how travel and sports have combined to bring me to places that most people only dream of. I love going back to New York at least once a year and soaking up the atmosphere and walking the streets to relive memories of my very early childhood and also of later years, after my father died and my mother and sisters returned to start afresh.

Before my father's tragically early death, when I was fifteen years old, I had an idyllic childhood in rural Co. Louth, in the Carlingford-Greenore area, about ten miles from Dundalk.

My father would be best described as a building engineer or mechanical engineer, and he did most of his technical work on the Cooley alcohol factory, which is now Cooley Distillery.

Before rural electrification, when the ESB put the poles up across the country, most households had paraffin lamps. My father, Lord have mercy on him, created his own wind-charger and electricity unit, and we had power pumped into our house long before anyone else had it. He had an amazing engineering brain, which I unfortunately don't possess. When I think of the man I think he must have been a genius in his own way.

First he built a base for the electricity unit; then he put a hole in the base, into which he fitted a pole that was about 25 to 30 feet high, and then filled in the base around it. I remember watching him then get a ladder and attach a dynamo to the top of the pole. He brought the dynamo up to the top, then reached into his pockets for all the screws and washers and tools— because he did all this single-handed, without any help. Down below he had batteries connected up to suck in the power from a propeller that rotated when the wind blew it.

Watching him at such a height I remember feeling nervous for him—and, to be honest, I don't think he fancied being up there in the first place. He had to tie up the propeller so it couldn't move in the breeze until he had fitted the batteries to take the power and feed it. When he had the batteries all linked up he went back up the ladder again, loosened the propeller, and descended. As soon as the wind blew we had power, and when the wind stopped we had reserve power from the batteries. I have to say I wish I had thought of telling him before he died that he was fantastic in being able to undertake such a challenge.

My mother used to wonder if I would ever be able to do anything with my hands. But I was the complete opposite of my father, who was so handy: he had the brain and the hands of an engineer, while his first-born son was bloody hopeless using his hands. Just to show how bad I am with my hands, I once made a clothes-horse in school, which had a dovetail joint, but when I had all the joints done and it was time to assemble it I discovered that one side was slightly higher than the other. I had to get the plane out to narrow it down, and of course then it was too much tilted the other way. This thing that started out at four foot high was suddenly two-and-a-half foot high. When I brought it home, my mother thought I was the bee's knees and was boastfully showing it off to all the neighbours. 'Look what my Jimmy made,' she said. Then one night she put a tea towel on it and the thing just collapsed. I think I decided there and then that I was not cut out to be a tradesman.

When we finally had electricity, I was amazed by the lights and particularly having a working radio switched on, listening intently to the sports programmes.

I was fascinated hearing Mícheál O'Hehir doing the

commentary for the 1947 all-Ireland final in New York, and I thought, 'Some day, I'm going to do that.' And I made my mind up there and then that this was it for me, and nothing was going to derail me or detour me from becoming a sports commentator.

Apart from O'Hehir, in those early days my broadcasting idols would have been the likes of Stewart MacPherson, John Arlott, and Raymond Glendenning, who worked with the BBC. They all helped bring out my passion for broadcasting and made me seriously think that I would like to do it.

I not only got to meet Mícheál O'Hehir but also got work from him when he was head of sport at RTE. When I was still a teenager I got my first taste of being on the radio when O'Hehir had me on a quiz one time. He had heard from someone who knew me that I was good at quizzes, and he invited me on to test my knowledge. Though it was my first time to be on radio, I wasn't nervous about speaking live on air, and in fact it felt innately natural. It was a fantastic experience. I remember O'Hehir firing off a couple of questions to test me, just for the fun of it, smiling and giving me the thumbs up when I impressed him with my quick and correct replies.

Looking back now, I don't know how I succeeded in getting into broadcasting, because nobody belonging to me was involved in broadcasting or in show business. I think my father's enthusiasm for sports rubbed off on me. He played a lot of football in New York, and in Cooley when he came home.

I fell so much in love with listening to the sports programmes that by the time I was seven or eight I began to do my own imaginary programmes. Everybody thought I was stone mad. I can only imagine what people made of this boy walking through the local fields doing an imaginary sports programme with 'live' commentary—and music to accompany it, because I also wanted to be a disc jockey.

I would do this programme without fail every time I was visiting my grandfather, who lived on the side of a mountain. It was a journey that would often take me an hour to make, even though he lived only thirty minutes away from us, because I would be so wrapped up in my show. I was always 'broadcasting'—or you could call it 'narrowcasting'. I had names, league tables, full reports; I would even change my voice when pretending to be a legendary sports figure being interviewed on my show.

On my walk to my grandfather's house I could get lost if I had a few extra reports to do, something like 'And now let's go to Dunedin to find out how the rugby test match is going. The New Zealand out-half' (whoever it was at the time) 'is suffering from an injury.'

How I laugh now when I think about it! But I loved it. Now that I look back on it, it was actually great experience for when I finally got in front of a microphone.

One of the local people heard me doing my imaginary show and said, 'That boy should write to Radio Éireann and look for an audition.' I was about eleven years old at the time, and I didn't even know what 'audition' meant; my mother had to look it up in the dictionary for me. I didn't really know what I was doing, but I got out the pen and paper and I wrote to Radio Éireann asking for my chance.

I didn't mention how young I was, but it had to be obvious from my childish penmanship; but it didn't stop them sending a curt reply, along the lines of 'Sorry, we have no vacancies at the moment, but we will put your name on file'—the usual brush-off reply.

On another occasion another neighbour, who was involved in athletics, stopped me and enquired, 'So, you think you can do athletics commentary?'

'Not really,' I modestly replied, before cryptically adding, 'I've done several, but I've never done any!'

My imagination was so good that I knew in my heart that I could do it. 'I'll do a mile race for you right now, if you like,' I said. At that time the four-minute barrier still hadn't been broken, before Roger Bannister broke the world record. Amused by the confidence oozing from me, he watched as I started off, staring into space, and gave the commentary on a mile race—with no watch or anything like tapes of races running to recite—and I finished at four minutes and two seconds.

'How did you do that?' he asked, amazed.

'I could just see them running the race in my imagination,' I explained, and then I continued on my journey with yet another imaginary radio show.

I was obsessed with sports to such an extent that I wrote letters to footballers. I don't know if children still do that these days, writing away to famous players. But I wrote to a who's who of English footballers of that era: Stanley Mathews, Wilf Mannion, Raich Carter, Tommy Lawton, Tom Finney. I suppose it was a childish thing—and all the letters were written in childish language, with bad spelling and grammar—but I wanted football tips, and I would ask them questions like 'How do you this trick?' and 'How do you do that particular defensive block?' and 'How do you make the ball swerve?' Or 'How do you get off your marker when somebody is marking you tight?' The letters would be a single page only, because I realised early on that nobody would get to a second page when reading such letters.

Sadly, I never got a reply from any of them. I had been giving these letters to my mother to post, so perhaps she never posted them—but I didn't know that: innocence is great—and that's probably the reason why I never got a reply.

My father, in cahoots with a neighbour, decided to play a prank on me. One day I received a letter—and I had never received a letter in my life. I remember with trembling hands looking at this letter addressed to Master James Magee. As I opened it I wondered who was writing to me; but the thrill quickly vanished when I discovered to my horror that it was from the head office of the GAA, and it went something like 'It has come to our attention that you have been writing to stars of cross-channel football. You would be better served making contact with the great people who play our own Gaelic games, such as Eddie Boyle,' etc. It was signed 'Yours faithfully, Pádraig Ó Caoimh,' who was the general secretary of the GAA at the time.

'How did they find out about my letters?' I pondered out loud. I was very worried, because I was sure my father, who was ill at the time, would be upset about how I had put shame on the family with my letter-writing carry-on. I must have looked really worried, because after a while my father enquired, 'What's wrong, Jimmy?'

I was too worried to tell him, but he persisted. 'You don't seem yourself. Are you all right?'

Nervously, I opened my mouth, and the whole story poured out. Taking the official-looking letter from me, which I subsequently learnt my neighbour Willie Lowe had got his wife to type, he pretended to examine it before exclaiming, 'God! That's unbelievable.' He would have made an excellent actor. Later, Willie and his wife dropped by, and the letter was brought up. After they all enjoyed winding me up—without punishing me too much—I was told the truth, and they broke out in laughter.

I eventually got to meet one of my sports heroes, although not a soccer-player, when the undisputed world flyweight champion, Rinty Monaghan of Belfast, visited my home town when I was twelve years old. He had arrived in Carlingford to visit some friends, and I rushed out looking for him when I heard the exciting news. There was no television back then, but I felt I had 'watched' all Rinty's fights when I listened on the wireless.

He was a fantastic character. When he won his fights, sometimes in London and sometimes in Belfast, he would stand up in the ring and sing for the audience, usually 'When Irish Eyes Are Smiling'. No matter what condition he was in, he sang; after he had done it a few times the crowd expected it. He was a good singer, and even made records.

When I saw him up close in the flesh I was struck by how much smaller than me he was, and I a boy only reaching his teens. I made my way through the crowd and brazenly introduced myself as he was going into a pub. 'My name is Jimmy Magee, and one day I'm going to do commentary on boxing.'

'I hope you do, I hope you do. Keep at it,' he replied in his strong Belfast accent. It was the usual uninspiring advice, but in fairness to him I must add that he stopped and chatted to me for a few minutes. In its own way it was inspirational. Here was a real live world champion, Rinty Monaghan—the first world champion I ever met.

He gave me his autograph before disappearing into the packed bar. It was one of the very few autographs I picked up over the years. Though later as a broadcaster, interviewing so many legendary sports figures, I would have the opportunity to pick up autographs, I just wasn't interested. In fact I only ever asked two people for their autograph—Pelé and Maradona—

when I went on a 'world tour' in 1977 to visit many of the sports landmarks that had made a lasting impression on me.

My parents also instilled in me a love of music, which I have to this day, and in fact in later years I was involved in a record company and wrote several songs. My mother could sing a good song; she wasn't a pro singer, but she was a good amateur singer. She didn't sing at céilithe or anything like that: she just knew a lot of songs and could sing them well. I learnt a lot of old songs from her, but she didn't sing them to teach me: I just picked them up, songs like 'Teddy O'Neill' and 'I'll Take You Home Again, Kathleen'.

My father played the accordion and was a musician of fairly high quality. He would perform locally with a little group of fellows, which was more like a jam session, in houses and sometimes in the pubs. I heard him play in the house a lot. I used to say to him that he was a fantastic musician, but he didn't think he was great and would instead list off the names of those musicians he held in high esteem. He continued to play until his health started to go.

He preferred Irish music, but he could play anything. The accordion was a big, heavy instrument. He got it specially made for him and it had *Magee* embossed down the front of it on the key side. It was a button-keyed accordion, which makes a big difference. A button-keyed accordion plays a different note in and out, which makes it more difficult to play. Dermot O'Brien, a late friend of mine, found it hard to perform on the old button-keyed accordion, because it was a different system.

One day when I was eight or nine my father was going somewhere and he left the accordion in the house. My mother told me not to touch it, but I went over to it anyway, because I was fascinated by it. It had what looked like ivory keys, and I started pressing them and began to play a tune. Haltingly, a tune came out: 'Boolavogue'. I couldn't lift the accordion, so it was still on the floor, and I could only go on playing for a certain bit of time. I deeply regret that I didn't learn how to play properly. I can play notes with my right hand but I can't play chords, and I can't play the bass. I was fascinated by how my father could play all the chords and how you put the keys together and where you put your fingers.

But sport was always my main passion. And even though, as I told my new boxing friend Rinty Monaghan, I passionately loved sports commentary, my main dream was to be a professional footballer, though truthfully I wasn't talented enough. I was playing sports every spare minute. I played a lot of football, but not hurling, because it wasn't really popular in my area. I don't suppose there would have been a single hurley stick in that part of Co. Louth at the time. And of course in my imagination I played for every team in the world that I described in my sports commentaries. I always ensured that a young Jimmy Magee scored the winning goal in injury time.

Any aspirations I had to play football professionally were killed off completely when, at the age of sixteen, I received a nasty knee injury while trying out for Dundalk. Even though I hurt the knee during the trial, I told myself, 'I'm not going to let this stop me.' I continued going, because I felt this was my big chance to shine. But the pain was horrendous, and they eventually had to bandage the knee up for me. I wasn't sent for an operation, and it did clear up eventually, but that was the end of my ambition to play professionally. I played a few minor matches with the injury, and I still don't know how I managed to put up with it. But even when it did clear up eventually it was never enough for me to take part in a real football match.

I decided then that one thing certain was that commentators lasted longer than players, which is true. I don't know where I got that wisdom from at such an early age, but I was right—as I'm still going strong to this day.

Chapter 2

WORK AND MARRIAGE

My idyllic childhood was shattered the day my father died in 1949 at the early age of forty-three, from pulmonary tuberculosis. Overnight I was forced to leave school and become 'the man of the house' and put food on the table for my mother, who, to make matters worse, was pregnant at the time of my father's death with my younger sister.

I can't recall how long my father had TB, a contagious bacterial infection that attacks the lungs, but it must have been for a considerable time, even though he never said he was suffering from it. He was seriously ill and bedridden only for a short time, maybe a year at most. I visited him every day. In retrospect, I'm amazed at how he managed to remain a very upbeat man despite the fact that he was suffering and was at death's door. He must surely have known he wasn't long for this world, and yet he found the courage to remain cheerful in front of me. Perhaps he didn't want to upset me, but we never had a conversation about the fact that he was dying.

There was always someone in the house to visit him— doctors, nurses, priests and lots of friends—as my father was a well-liked man.

He was a great man for the advertisements and testimonials promising cures in the newspapers. He would read them out to me and say, 'Ah, I have to get that, Jimmy. Will you be a good lad and run down to the chemist and see can you get that for me? Thanks, son.'

I can't remember how many times I came back with some of these so-called cures, but I remember the pharmacist one day asking me when I went in to order the latest remedy, 'Who's that for?'

'My father,' I replied.

'It will do him no good, you know.'

'Well, he thinks it will.'

'Ah, well, if he thinks it will do him good it will do him good.'

I remember my last conversation with my father. It wasn't really a conversation as much as him telling me, 'You're the man of the house now, Jimmy.'

I remember thinking during this poignant conversation, 'I'm going to be some man of the house at fifteen years old!'

Then he said: 'Whatever you do, look after your mother, Jimmy. Make no mistakes: just look after her. And of course you can't look after her unless you look after yourself first.'

'I promise,' I told him, choking back the tears.

I found it difficult with everyone looking at me in that room and listening to everyone telling me that I was the man of the house now. But the advice my father gave me was really great advice. My mother thought the sun shone out of me.

Shortly after the last time we spoke, my father passed away during the night. I knew he wasn't long for the world when I saw my uncle arriving with the parish priest. Outside the bedroom I listened to the faint mumblings of the priest reading my father the last rites.

My uncle, my mother's brother, was very kind to me and kept saying to me that I would be the man of the house soon, preparing me for the worst. Eventually he came out of the bedroom and came over to me. 'Jimmy, it's happened,' he told me.

With my eyes welling up, I went up to the bedroom and I looked at my dead father. I was devastated. It was a massive shock to lose my father when I was still only a teenager. But I can't even begin to imagine how difficult it must have been for my mother, now expecting her fourth child. During the ordeal she was always very good with us, but I suppose we were also good to her and making sure we never gave her any trouble, because it was obvious that she could do without it. If she said to us, 'Don't do that,' we wouldn't, because what would have been the point in annoying the poor woman?

All the neighbours thought, 'Jaysus! This is the end of the world. Sure this young fella won't be able to mind them.' But in fact I was able to look after my mother, and become a father figure to my two sisters, Mary and Patricia. It's amazing how you can find the strength and determination in such adversity.

I was now head of the household, and any plans and ambitions I had went out the window. I had to leave school, a decision that was made very reluctantly, because I had always been passionate about my education. I decided I would do the matriculation, though it was hard studying at home at night-time and I wasn't really able to keep up with it, because I was too tired after I started in a job.

Soon after my father died some of his friends informed me that they had heard about a job going for someone to serve their time as a pharmacist in Carlingford. I applied for the job and got it, probably as a result of my father's friends having a word with the proprietor. My mind was made up then—I'm very single-minded when I put my mind to something—to settle down to a career as a pharmacist, because at the very least I would have a good qualification.

I started off on the pittance of £1 a week, out of which I got one shilling and gave the rest to my mother for feeding us all. Now you would get little enough for twenty shillings, which was the equivalent of a pound, and feck-all for one shilling; however, even though the money wasn't great it did put food on the table. There wasn't a lot of food, but it was enough to keep everyone from starving.

We grew our own potatoes and vegetables. We used to get clothes and parcels from family members in America, which was a great help. I would be dressed in these hand-me-down suits, which were beautiful but at the same time the most outlandish suits, of a kind that you couldn't get in Ireland. I thought they were fantastic, but my friends used to say I looked like Al Capone.

I stuck it out at the pharmacy bravely enough for nearly two years. I walked the two miles there and two miles back until I got an old ramshackle bike. However, I knew I had to get a job with better pay, and when I was seventeen I applied for a position in British Railways (later called British Rail), along with, I suppose, every other able-bodied person in the district. At the time the company had an extension to the Dundalk, Newry and Greenore Railway, which became part of the Great Northern Railway somewhere along the way. Luckily, I got one of the jobs at something like £4 a week, and the extra money made a big difference for us.

However, I was only in the place six months when it closed down. I hate hearing people saying today, 'Ah, the country's in ruins.' It was actually worse in the 1950s, and we didn't die. It was an awful shock to hear that I could be out of a job, but thankfully I was one of six people who survived the cull, and I was transferred to offices in Dublin. I was eighteen, and I thought it was the beginning of a new life and was determined to pursue my dream of becoming a sports commentator and getting to meet all my heroes.

I moved to digs in Fairview while working with British Railways as a clerk. I was miserable doing the job. I suppose the digs were all right, but I missed having my family around me. I got a bit more than my £4 a week, with a removal allowance, which made life easier; and whatever money was left after my living expenses and the digs was sent home.

Most fellows I worked with were thinking of how some day they could be the stationmaster at Dundalk or piermaster at Dún Laoghaire, but that never entered my head: I was still dreaming of getting my foot into the world of broadcasting.

I became friends with a colleague in the company's North Wall office named Peter Byrne, who would go on to become one of our finest sports journalists. We were both in the Passenger and Import Office, and all the goods came through us. Peter and I both began to do freelance bits and pieces while working there, he for the *Evening Press* and the *Evening Mail* while I managed to get my foot into Radio Éireann. It's funny how we both ended up in the media; Peter is now president and I'm vice-president of the Association of Sports Journalists in Ireland. Peter and I sometimes have a laugh about how we both ended up in journalism; after all, he could just as easily have been the piermaster in Dún Laoghaire—and I could have been the train-driver.

Peter likes to tell a story about our time working together in British Railways, which he calls the elephant story, because, as people say, an elephant never forgets. Naturally, he always blames me, and *vice versa,* for this comedy of errors of misplacing a road roller, which county councils use for rolling tar on roads. This road roller came in and we checked it in, and whoever was putting it away put it against the gable end of the shed, which is where the hay for the horses was being kept. The hay was eventually piled up around it.

When Meath County Council came to collect it, it couldn't be found, even though it was checked in on the manifest. After a long and exhaustive search it still couldn't be found. Months and months went by and we were still unable to track it down, with the result that compensation was paid.

One day someone was getting hay for the horses and they saw a funnel sticking out. They investigated, only to discover this phantom road roller that had been hidden away for almost a year.

If you're reading this, Peter, I still don't believe it was my fault!

———

It was truly a case of love at first sight when I first met Marie Gallagher in 1953. I was only about eighteen and was newly arrived in Dublin. I fell head over heels immediately after first noticing this beautiful brunette with a beguiling smile and warm laugh at a ballroom beside the Gate Theatre, but I have to be completely honest and add that she was probably nonplussed about me and that it took a lot of effort and charm for me to win Marie over.

Even though she didn't jump at my propositions for a while, I continued charming her until she relented and agreed to dance with me. I was taken by her jovial personality. In truth I had always been—and still am—attracted to women with a smiling face. Marie's smile from that night is still etched in my memory. When I finally got to know her well I discovered that she had a tremendous cheerful personality; she was someone who was always jolly and never became grumpy. I would jokingly tell her years later that grumpiness appeared in her demeanour only after years of her patience being tested by yours truly.

I didn't get to walk her home that night to Crumlin: I quickly realised that was not going to be part of the scheme when Marie told me she was being chaperoned by her sister (who has also sadly passed away). I didn't get the opportunity to ask Marie out properly that night, but before we parted she let it slip that she would be attending a party later on in the week.

I couldn't get her out of my mind, and I decided to gate-crash this party. I didn't even want to go to the party; I desperately wanted to ask Marie out. Anyway, I arrived at the bash and I remember the men there giving me—this total stranger who had the audacity to attempt to barge into a private party to chase a woman—a frosty reception.

'Yeah, what do you want?' one of the fellows asked me at the door.

I told them Marie Gallagher was expecting me, though of course she wasn't. Eventually she came out, and I asked her for a date. I think she must have taken pity on me!

We went to the cinema on our first date—where else would you go in the mid-1950s? I might be known as the Memory Man, but for the life of me I can't remember what film we went to see. It may have been *Blackboard Jungle,* or something like that, as it was the beginning of rock and roll when I first met Marie. I wasn't all that interested in the film anyway: I only had eyes for Marie! Thankfully, I must have done something right to impress her that night, because she agreed to another date after I walked her home. We soon became inseparable and began to regularly attend shows in the Theatre Royal, which had a variety bill that included the top acts of the time, like

Danny Kaye and Frankie Laine. Marie was a huge cinema fan, but I was never really into films, and I haven't been to that many since those early days of our courtship.

Within two years we decided to get married. I was probably tempting fate, and I can't believe it now, looking back all these years later, that I was only twenty when we got married. I was far too young for such a lifetime commitment; but as it turned out it was the best thing ever to happen to me. Marie was my bedrock, and getting married matured me and spurred me on with my career ambitions.

Besides, back in those days it was completely unheard of for couples to be living together—'living in sin', as it was called—or having an intimate relationship before walking down the aisle. It amazes me now when I think of how times have changed to such an extent that today's generation can do what they like without being frowned upon. Young people will probably have a giggle reading about how in my day if you wanted to advance your relationship the only way forward was marriage.

I was a nervous wreck asking Marie for her hand in marriage. I did my best to be romantic. I wanted to tell her, 'I can't live without you', but I hadn't got the courage then to say something so profound. Instead I found the words stumbling clumsily out of my mouth as I walked her home. 'We'll have to stop meeting like this! Why don't we get married?' I said, kicking myself because I hadn't the courage to be more romantic. I was relieved when Marie readily agreed, and I embraced her and told her how much I loved her.

Later that week I was very nervous when I went out to Marie's home to ask her father, Daniel, for his permission to ask her to marry me.

'Hello, Mr Gallagher,' I began anxiously. 'I'd like to ask you something.'

'Sure I know what you want to ask me,' he replied.

'There's no point in asking so,' I gingerly answered, smiling.

'No, go on and ask me anyway.'

'Would you have the loan of a tenner?' I joked.

'Now, Jimmy, sure that's not what you were going to ask me at all! And anyway, if it was, is that all you're going to spend on her?'

We both laughed, and then I formally asked him.

It all happened very quickly after that, and on 11 October 1955 Marie was walking down the aisle in a beautiful white dress in St Agnes' Church, Crumlin.

For our honeymoon we went to London, and we spent our time enjoying ourselves at the theatres and eating out. We went to a West End show starring Benny Hill and Norman Wisdom. Marie couldn't stop laughing, and the more she laughed the more Wisdom accentuated his performance. He got one of the ushers to come to get Marie after the show and bring her down to meet him; he asked her where she would be for the next show! She always thought Norman Wisdom was the greatest thing since sliced bread.

When we got married I was no longer able to send the few bob to my mother. Many years later she told me she was very grateful that I had continued sending money home as long as I had done. Besides, by that time my two sisters were old enough to fend for themselves, and this meant that my mother could go back out to work. She and my sisters decided that they wanted to return to New York and begin afresh there, as many of my uncles and aunts were still living there. I was probably taken aback by the decision, but I was also happy for them, even though I knew that I would soon miss them here in Ireland.

My mother had a real bond with America and truly loved it over there. She told me: 'When I was in America I loved Ireland, but when I was in Ireland I loved America.' I'm a bit like her in that regard. I never realised it until now, but she had probably waited until I was semi-settled before she made her own move back to New York, which is something I would thank her for now if she was still with us. I think she may have suggested at one time that I might consider moving back to the place of my birth, but I didn't want to go: I wanted to carve out a career in broadcasting here.

On the day they were all going back over I thought to myself, 'I'm the only one born in America and I'm now the only one of us living in Ireland, which is a bit of an unusual twist.'

We had the perfect start to our marriage. After we returned from London we moved into a lovely little house in Dalkey, which we rented for three or four years. Even though it was one of the nicest places I have ever had, I decided that there was no way we could raise a family in this small place, which was covered from top to bottom with my collection of books. I was very interested in travelling and geography and would always be coming back home with books and city maps of places like Chicago and New York. When I'd arrive home with a bundle of books under my arm Marie would sigh, shake her head and ask me, 'What are you going to do with all the books?'

'I'm going to travel to all these places,' I would reply, and I'd list off the various countries I was dreaming about visiting.

'Not at all. That will never happen.'

I vowed to her that it would happen. She probably thought I was a mad dreamer, but she was thrilled when I proved her wrong.

Happily, Marie never really minded me travelling on my own. But it made no difference to me at the time as, if truth be known, I was going regardless, because I was determined to advance my career. Perhaps it was somewhat selfish of me, but

I never really stopped to ask if she minded me going away—but at the same time it wasn't as if I was going on holidays: I think Marie understood that it was, after all, for work and to put food on our table.

But even though I enjoyed seeing the world and witnessing at first hand some of the most important and iconic moments in twentieth-century sporting history, as well as the stars themselves, I did often become homesick and miss the family. Hotel rooms can be lonely places.

Luckily, however, I was mostly around when our first children were infants, as I was only getting my foot in the door of broadcasting then and hadn't yet begun to skedaddle off and travel around the world to cover events.

| BREAKTHROUGH

While working in British Railways I was itching to get my shot at broadcasting. I decided to again write an audition letter to Radio Éireann—though in a more professional-looking manner than my childish squiggles at the age of eleven.

In May 1956 I finally got an audition for a new programme beginning at the time, which was to be called 'Junior Sports Magazine'. It was to be presented by Harry Thuillier, who was one of Ireland's biggest radio stars at the time—almost like his generation's Larry Gogan or Gerry Ryan. The show also had some top sports reporters, such as Seán Diffley, Fred Cogley, Tony Sheehan and Leo Nealon, names that meant something back then. I had pestered Harry, who had represented Ireland in two Summer Olympics in fencing, by constantly phoning him, looking for my break. I must have worn him down, because he eventually rang me back and told me to come up for a voice test.

Two or three days after my audition my life dramatically changed when I received a phone call from Harry. 'We listened back to that; it was quite good for a newcomer. Will you do a report and commentary on a game for us on Saturday?'

I was slightly nervous doing my first report, but I knew what I was doing. Also, without being cocky about it, hadn't I done it so often in my own head, walking around the fields? So I told myself there was no problem.

Afterwards Harry invited me to work on the show as a freelance; and it was simply the best feeling in the world to finally be doing something I had dreamt about ever since I was a boy sitting in front of the wireless listening to that memorable all-Ireland final from New York.

'Junior Sports Magazine' was a great learning experience, because when you came in with your written report you also brought in your commentary tape, and you spliced the tape down in the editing suite for broadcasting. I had to present them every week with about one-and-a-half minutes of commentary. Though I didn't realise it at the time, it was like a training school.

It was also great learning to work on a shoestring budget. Radio Éireann once sent me to the White City in London to cover the Emsley Carr Mile, which was a famous athletics event at the time. It was the first appearance of Herb Elliott in Britain, the man who was eventually to break the 3.55 for the mile.

When I arrived at the event I was asked, 'Have you a producer?' to which I answered, 'I'm the producer!'

I was then asked, 'Have you a statistician?'

'You're looking at him. I'm the statistician.'

And the BBC were there with their big team: Harold Abrahams, who featured in 'Chariots of Fire', was one of the commentators; Rex Alston; two producers; race readers; timekeepers. I was the entire Radio Éireann team! I was paid a bit extra each week for doing all the tasks, and I did it as well as the BBC team.

My first big interview on the show was with the golfer Arnold Palmer when the Canada Cup, today known as the

World Cup of Golf, was held in Portmarnock in 1960. It's a competition that's probably best described as two-man teams representing their own countries. The American team that year had two giants of the golf world, Sam Snead, who won three Masters, three PGA and one British Open, and Arnold Palmer, who is generally regarded as one of the greatest professional players in the history of the sport, having won seven major championships—in fact *Golf Digest* in 2007 ranked him in sixth place of the all-time greats, an amazing feat when you begin to think about the pantheon of great golfers.

At the time Snead was the older of the two and the big figure of the day. Even though Palmer had won the British Open in 1960, he was still perceived as 'the coming-along boy'.

I was sent out to get an interview with Snead for 'Junior Sports Magazine'. I asked Snead and he was less than forthcoming, almost dismissive. I was beginning to wonder what I would do when Palmer came over and said he would do an interview for me. He was being called to tee off, but he told me, 'Come with me.'

We walked together up to the tee and recorded a five-minute interview there. For him to do that for somebody who was of no benefit to him at the time was a very nice thing to do. There was an old priest I served Mass for when I was an altar boy who taught me, 'You judge a man by how he treats those who can do nothing for him,' which is a lovely saying. It's an adage that sums up Palmer's affable and generous character. To this day, particularly in the light of what a legend Palmer later became, it is one of my fondest memories, being out there doing an interview as he prepared to tee off.

I mentioned to Palmer when I met him on a couple of other occasions that it was my first big interview, which always put a smile on his face.

'Junior Sports Magazine' was a very good programme, which I thought would go on indefinitely, but sadly it abruptly ended in the late 1960s when, as the cliché goes, television killed the radio star. I stayed on until its final broadcast.

Harry had me running around every weekend doing all the matches nobody else wanted to do. He got me to go out one day to do a women's hockey match out by Ballsbridge. I couldn't believe my ears when he told me, 'I want you to go to the dressing-room and interview one of the winning players—'

'But,' I interjected, 'this is a women's final!'

Even though it was unheard of at the time for a member of the opposite sex to go into the dressing-room, and it still wouldn't happen often, Harry insisted. I didn't want to do it, but at the same time I knew I had to comply with his orders if I wanted to continue working on the show.

Nervously, I went out to the game. I approached one woman whom I knew who played centre-forward for Pembroke. I explained the position I was in, and she told me not to worry, that she would come to me 'in the little alcove afterwards, and we'll do the interview,' which she did.

In fairness to Harry, who I suppose was my first boss in RTE, he became a mentor to me. He was a big influence on my career and I liked him a lot. Harry and I often worked together, but nobody really pushed me: I'd like to think I achieved it all on my own talent, to be honest. I wouldn't like to be in debt to someone for any reason like that. I was a bit conscious of being young, inexperienced and maybe even gullible in the early days, so it was great to have Harry by my side.

After I had got my foot in the door of Radio Éireann, my first child, Paul, was born in January 1957. Tragically, he was to die at the age of forty-nine from motor neurone disease. I remember the day he was born very well and people commenting to me, 'Sure how could you be a father? You're only a child yourself!'

Shortly after Paul was born I received some unexpected news. It was something that I never dwelt on, but I knew deep down that my mother must have been very lonely for all those years without male companionship. When she was out on her own again in New York the inevitable happened and she met someone else and fell in love and decided to get married again. He was an Irishman called Gerry Byrne, who was a few years younger than her. She probably picked an Irishman because she didn't trust any other nationalities!

I did like the man she married, which helped me come to terms with it all. My mother took his name, which also took me time to adjust to. When I heard about it all I joked that she did nothing but change her name! Unfortunately, I didn't go over for the wedding; it was a small private wedding. I probably would have found it to be an emotionally difficult wedding to attend, as I imagine that painful memories of my beloved father would probably have crept into my mind; but I couldn't go because of the convenient excuse of work commitments. I think my mother was slightly disappointed, but she told me she understood. However, in retrospect I'm annoyed with myself for not making more of an effort to be there for her. I might have been contracted to do something and felt I had to do it, but of course now I know that if you need to get out of something you can usually get out of it.

Regardless of my initial discomfort with my mother remarrying, it proved to be a strong relationship, and they remained together up to her death. Gerry is still alive and is still over in New York, though we haven't been in touch for a long time. I never severed the connection, but we just haven't kept in contact. But I will always be grateful to him for making my mother a happy woman again.

————

Two-and-a-half years after Paul was born my eldest daughter, Linda (who probably won't appreciate me giving away her age) was the next to arrive, in 1959. Linda, an excellent dancer, from ballet to pop, has devoted most of her adult life to being a professional teacher on all aspects of the art of dance. We then had two more beautiful girls: June, who was born in 1962, quickly followed by Patricia, who arrived in 1963. The baby of the family, my second son, Mark, was born in 1970. By the time he arrived we were already living in rented accommodation in Stillorgan, but with five children it was going to be too cramped, so I decided finally to get a mortgage and we moved to a large house, with a lovely back garden, in the same area.

The atmosphere in our house was brilliant when the children were growing up. The family was pretty close-knit; we all got on well, which was great, and enjoyed being in each other's company. I believe parenthood is the only job in the world with no training for it. It's a big responsibility, but I thoroughly enjoyed it. I think they all have fond memories of their childhood, and I hope they have no bad memories, which is the way I think it should be. They wouldn't have any memories of shouting or roaring, which is scary for children, I think. I never hit my children but they might have been threatened if they stepped out of line. They didn't need a slap as a threat, as using an admonishing voice usually worked: it was normally enough for me to say, 'Don't do that again,' because they were generally well-behaved and respectful children.

We went loads of places together and we had a lot of fun in all its forms. But when I reflect on my memories of raising my children my mind always wanders back fondly to the times I had with the five children in our back garden. They were all interested in sports, and we used to have fantastic games out in the garden. It was as if everything had gone full circle: here I was in fatherhood doing what I had done as a kid, pretend commentary and playing imaginary games all over again with my own children. We would pretend our back garden was Croke Park at the all-Ireland final, or Wembley for the FA cup final, or whatever city happened to be holding the final.

Now, our back garden was modest in size, but even still we would find the space to play those magical games. Paul and I would be the two captains, and we would have comical rows, giving out to each other in jest.

There's no doubt that, just as I did, my children derived their own love of sport from me, as I did from my father; but, unlike me, they all went on to become quite accomplished at different sports. Paul went on to play professional football and won a League Cup medal with Shamrock Rovers in 1977. Growing up, they all played hockey or camogie, and they all bowled to a fairly high degree of proficiency. Patricia once held the record for the number of pins dropped in the European Championship. All of them have remarkably low single-figure handicaps in golf. Paul was down to a handicap of a mere six when he took ill.

In a very interesting double, Patricia won the captain's prize in Kiltiernan, and when the club broke up she moved to Coolattin, Co. Wicklow, and years later she won the captain's prize there too. June also won the captain's prize at Coolattin. So they won three captain's prizes in two years, which was amazing. I was very proud of them both.

My younger son, Mark, who is one of my best friends, is also a very good golfer in single handicap, but he doesn't often get the time to play, because of family and work commitments.

In fact they all played better than me, who, typically enough, was the odd one out. I was an avid golfer until I discovered one day that I wasn't getting any better at it, so I gave it up. Nobody could believe that I just stopped playing, but it was annoying me that I wasn't getting any better. In truth I thought that, rather than improving, my game was in decline. 'I'm getting brutal,' I thought one morning as I missed yet another putt that I had visualised sinking perfectly, and I decided I was better off sticking to what I knew best: being a sports fan who was lucky enough to be able to give his opinions over the airwaves.

Chapter 4

GOING PROFESSIONAL

After a few years of freelancing with Radio Éireann I took the plunge and decided to give up my pensionable job at British Railways. Perhaps my boss was relieved to see the back of me, because I probably wasn't the best timekeeper in the world. I was always rushing off on radio assignments or going into Radio Éireann's editing suite, which was in the GPO at the time.

I would never have made the big move without the support of Marie. I assured her that I wouldn't let her down. 'I know I can do it if I could get a chance,' I reassured her. A lot of the successes I had enjoyed up till then were because I made my own chances. I'm a firm believer that you make your own luck in this life.

Funnily enough, when I went to Radio Éireann full-time I ended up being the best timekeeper I know. At British Railways, if 9:10 a.m. was your starting time they would draw a red line, and if you were underneath that line you were a 'big late boy'. They would have given me a small bit of trouble for my tardiness as I juggled my full-time job with my freelance broadcasting work on 'Junior Sports Magazine'.

It was a dream to go full-time as a freelance with Radio Éireann, but it was a hard time to give up the British Railways job, because it was guaranteed money for life—a pensionable job, which was the dream of everyone at the time. I must have been either silly or confident—and maybe a little of each, if truth be known—to leave it for the precarious world of freelancing at Radio Éireann.

'Junior Sports Magazine' paid £1.50 a week, and then for sponsored programmes you got maybe £3 or £4 a week. If you put these all together you could get a decent living—provided the programme stayed on the air. I was making more than I had in British Railways; but it could all fall apart in the blink of an eye if the sponsor pulled the plug because they ran out of money, or the contract might be up and they wouldn't renew. Thankfully, I was mostly working, but there was the odd occasion in those early years when work dried up.

I found everyone at Radio Éireann in those days to be quite nice and even taking pity on this young fella Jimmy Magee. They couldn't believe it when I arrived in one day with a couple of children with me. I was asked, 'Are they yours?' They probably thought they should start giving me a bit of work when it dawned on them that I was a married man with commitments (though that wasn't the reason I brought the children in).

Luckily, I was always able to come up with ideas for sponsored programmes. I was familiar with all the workings of the fifteen-minute sponsored programme. It's like writing a song: you have to have a hook that will grab them. If I may say so, I was good at it. I would come up with an idea, and the sponsor would usually love it. And most of the stuff I did was done through Harry Thuillier, who was brilliant at pitching ideas to sponsors.

Even though the sports programme was hugely successful, Harry wasn't satisfied with just one thing: he always had to think of something else to do. Harry was a brilliant broadcaster, and this was because he was innovative and would always think up some fantastic ideas for new shows we could propose to Radio Éireann and the sponsors. We would make a presentation to the powers that be in RE, and if they approved and gave us a time slot we could then seek a sponsor to give us a budget for the show and basically pay our wages.

The period from 8 to 10 a.m. was split into fifteen-minute segments, the same at lunchtime and the same at night, so RE had this space available, and the advertising agencies would come to RE's commercial department and book fifteen minutes for their clients. RE would have to get a programme for them; the programme in turn would have to meet the RE guidelines.

We used to do a programme for one of the sweets manufacturers, and on it we gave a guinea or two (£1.05 or £2.10) for spotting our deliberate mistake. I was in the studio pressing the buttons and Harry was doing the programme, and he made a lot of mistakes—and the programme was live. So I said to him, 'Harry, you're going to be in trouble delivering the prize today.'

'Don't worry about it. If it comes to that point I'll say, "Well, I know I made a lot of mistakes today, but did you spot the *deliberate* one?"'

Who else could get away with that?

Afterwards Harry said that we needed to come up with another idea for a show to pitch to Tayto Crisps for the next morning! 'Jimmy, you're the ideas man. You must have something in your brain.'

I told him to leave it with me; I was sure I would come up with something. We arranged to meet at ten the following morning to go out together to meet the managing director of Tayto. I kept racking my brains the whole way out there. We met, and I still hadn't a solid idea. When we sat down at the meeting, Harry said to the managing director, 'Jimmy has a great idea!'

Making it up as I went along, I began to describe a very simple idea: a quiz show called the 'Tayto Family Show'. It ended up being one of our biggest successes. We recorded it in public places—clubs generally. I told them it would have a county theme, going stage by stage through the different counties, and the winners would then represent Ireland in the world championship.

I paused for effect. Harry was staring at me in bewilderment, wondering where this crazy idea had come from. I carried on explaining. 'We'll recruit the teams through the embassies in Dublin.' They thought it was a wonderful idea and, believe it or not, it took to the air: the Tayto International World Cup of Quiz! Looking back on it now, I think it was so far-fetched it's unbelievable.

We had no team from Nigeria, so Harry took it on himself to go down to Trinity College one evening. He saw a few African students walking around and went up to them and asked if they were busy that evening. If the reply was No he would then get them to go to the recording studio. They weren't from Nigeria at all—one was from Sierra Leone, someone from Liberia—but they ended up representing Nigeria! You wouldn't get away with such antics today.

We had a disaster with a short-lived programme sponsored by a watch company. Radio Luxembourg had a show at the time that was interspersed with the slogan 'And the time by my H. Samuel Ever-Right watch is . . .' Our programme was for Corona Watches, and for this I wrote the slogan 'The time now by my ever-correct Corona is . . .'

Now, the man who ran Corona Watches didn't care tuppence

about what music you played, as long as his product was plugged regularly. But we had a problem, which I quickly discovered during our first week on air. I said, 'And that was Frank Sinatra's "High Hopes". And the time now by my ever-correct Corona is . . .' and I paused for Harry to read the time but was instead met with nothing but dead air. Harry tried in vain to read the watch: 'Three minutes past a quarter to . . . seven minutes to . . . it's ten seconds past ten to . . . it's 2:45 and seven . . . ah, it's about ten to three.'

It turned out that Harry couldn't read the moving second hand!

We lost that programme because he couldn't give out the time to the second, as stipulated in the contract. I laugh at this story now, but it certainly wasn't a laughing matter at the time.

We then had a programme for Lucozade, visiting hospitals and interviewing patients, and we would play the patients' choice of music. It may not have been rocket science, but this was another of my ideas. We would do maybe three or four interviews and then play three or four records.

Harry always seemed to have as many shows as possible recorded—'for a rainy day,' as he would put it. But it was a method that got us into hot water.

'How many have we done?' he'd ask.

'We've done up to November.'

'Oh, you better do a few more, with Christmas coming up.'

Later he would ask again, 'How many shows have you in the bag now?'

I would tell him we were up to the 31st of December, but he insisted, 'We better do some more for a rainy day.'

It was the proverbial rainy day that landed us in hot water. One day the programme went out as usual—but some of the people interviewed on it were dead! We would say to the people when interviewing them, 'You're looking good! Does the doctor think you'll be out soon?' And they would answer, 'Yes,' or 'I hope so,' and you would say, 'Good luck,' and 'See you in the bar some time for a pint.' The interviews had been done about three months in advance. When this programme went out it was horrible and mortifying to discover that some of the people had passed away in the meantime; but it's also a little bit amusing looking back on it.

The boys called the show 'Come Die with Me'. This was a reference to a show Harry and I did together called 'Come Fly with Me', which was sponsored by Jacob's. He would begin by announcing something along the lines of 'Today we're flying from Dublin to Paris,' and he would go up and down the aisle of the plane interviewing people. It was a good idea, and Jacob's loved how he was bringing them up in the air.

One day the recording machine didn't work properly on the way to Paris, and Harry came back to discover that there was nothing on the tape. On the following trip he was going from Dublin to Rome, but he explained to the few passengers that when he would be talking to them they were to pretend they were *en route* to Paris! Some passengers didn't understand him and told the steward that he thought they were going to Paris when in fact they were going to Rome. He had the whole place in turmoil. It was hilarious.

Another time he was doing a handy run from Dublin to Manchester. He started with, 'And here I am speaking to three Manchurians,' but when he got back he was told that it was 'Mancunians'. That piece was unusable.

The next time he was going to Glasgow and he said, 'Here I am speaking to two Glas . . . two people from Glasgow.'

He was full of that sort of stuff, but he was gloriously funny and full of eternal youth.

Harry was a gambler both in his career and in his personal life. As a joke he would try to get my wages off me by tossing a coin. I hadn't got the money to gamble, because—as Harry knew full well—I had a wife and children to support.

One time he owed me £24, but he suggested tossing for it. I told him I couldn't afford to, but he persuaded me to. And then he called for double or quits—£48 or nothing . . . and I lost! It went on and on until the early hours of the morning, outside a pub near Holles Street. It was drizzling rain, and here we were tossing a coin.

'How much do I owe you now?' I asked him.

'£1,980. Will we go for one more toss?'

I began to tell him that I just wanted to go home; and the next thing is a squad car arrived. The nurses in the nurses' home beside Holles Street Hospital had obviously phoned the guards, because they thought we were having a serious row over money. The guards asked what we were at, and we explained to them that it was just a bit of fun.

Though I was flying with radio work, I didn't get an opportunity to do much television. The first real thing I did on television was the FA cup final in 1967 between Chelsea and Tottenham Hotspur, which Spurs won 2-1. The producer who went to that with me, Justin Nelson, was a lovely fellow and very helpful to me. He ended up being the producer of 'Superstars' on television, and with it we travelled to the Bahamas, Israel and the United States. Up to that point I would have done little pieces here and there—five minutes here and ten minutes there—but that was my first real television broadcast.

In the 1960s I was also involved in a radio programme called 'Spot the Talent'. It was an inter-county contest. It consisted of four acts: a singing act, a musical act, an instrument and a novelty act. Some talented people got their big break on the show, such as Matt Molloy of the Chieftains.

There were three judges, and it was always done live in the Francis Xavier Hall on a Monday evening. During the interval the Radio Éireann Light Orchestra would play, allowing the judges to come down onto the stage and appear in front of the audience and do their summing up. It was straightforward enough. One of the judges, Éamonn Ó Gallchobhair, was just like a blunt 'X Factor' judge, he was so cutting with the way he would deal with these amateurs—and that's what they were: only amateurs, who didn't deserve a tongue-lashing.

On this particular evening we arrived for the rehearsal, and on the stage were big banks of loudspeakers, which was surprising, because it was normally a bare stage, at most only a small amplifier for a guitar. But this stuff was massive. Then these four guys representing Cork came out onto the stage. Their lead guitarist was a long-haired fellow, and I thought to myself, 'Wait until Ó Gallchobhair gets at him with his honest criticism! What is he going to say?'

When Ó Gallchobhair came on he said: 'The young man who played the guitar—I think he was a young man anyway, because his hair was so long I'm surprised he didn't get it caught in the strings or anything else . . . I'm a long time in music of all kinds, and I've seen and heard them all, but I never before heard a young man with such phrasing and exquisite finger work and fret work. This man is a genius.'

Now this wasn't Éamonn's type of music at all. He was a classical musician, and this guy was playing rock. That young lad was Rory Gallagher. This story illustrates how good Rory was, and how much Éamonn knew about music, even if it wasn't his type of music.

Rory Gallagher was brilliant. I interviewed him on the show;

he was a lovely fellow and a very quiet man. You could hardly hear him talk, he was so shy.

I met him later on in his career when he played in the National Stadium, and I reminded him of that story; he told me he remembered that night well. I told him how fearful we were for him regarding what Ó Gallchobhair would say about him. 'But it showed just how great you were,' I added.

'I'm not great—not great yet, but I'm working on it,' he replied humbly. Rory was always working on perfection.

––––

My career wasn't all sweetness and light in those days. I was brought down to earth with a loud thump on a few occasions. Once in the late 1970s there was a guy in Dublin called Larry Finn, a West Indian. Larry's style of music was mainly calypso—not quite Jimi Hendrix, but it was calypso. He thought that if he got a break it would propel him into the big time; so he booked a little theatre in Westland Row and decided to do a Christmas season, and he asked me to MC it. There was one other act, Veronica Blanchfield, who did a 'Burlington Bertie from Bow' kind of act.

The plan was that it would run for three nights, and we took out advertisements in the *Evening Herald.* On the opening night you could feel the nervousness in the air. We were looking out through the curtains and Larry would be asking, 'Is there many in?'

To keep him calm I told him, 'Only about ten.'

'We'll give it another few minutes,' he replied.

I went out to open the show, and there were only two people in the audience. I introduced Veronica and—fair play to her—

she went out and did a little bit; and then I did a few stories, and then Larry came out. 'I want to interrupt Jimmy there,' he said. 'Do either of you gentlemen play the piano?'

One of them said he did, so Larry asked him to play with him, because he had no accompanist. The fellow came up to the stage, and the other fellow said, 'Listen, I'll see yeh afterwards in Kennedy's when the show is over.'

So now we had no audience! We did keep going, but we didn't do a second half. Larry collected five shillings (25p) for the whole show. He gave half to me and half to himself, and nothing to Veronica; but he bought her a mineral later in Kennedy's pub!

Harry and I remained friends until he passed away, but we stopped working together after a blazing row, and that was the end of it as a working partnership. I have never mentioned this before, but I got thick with him, and he was thick to begin with when on this particular morning we were recording in the ACT Studios in Mount Street. I had arrived with my scripts, which weren't great, because they were rushed. I had been up half the night writing stuff, as he was going away and he wanted to get a few things done. I was exhausted. I would say that some of the stuff was at least sub-standard. Harry had a cursory look through it while I was in the studio with the buttons. He was in the microphone studio with the microphone on when I heard him blast, 'Jesus! How could you read this shite? How could you read it?'

I was annoyed, because he damn well knew that I could hear him. I went into the studio and I grabbed the stuff and said, 'You won't have to read it for much longer, Harry.' And I took it and tore it. It was like tearing up a telephone book, it was that thick, but I could have torn the wall off. I tore it and tore it and then I threw it up like confetti and said, 'That's it . . . we're finished. No more scripts. No more nothing.' And I stormed out.

'Jimmy! Jimmy!' He began calling after me to come back, but I told him that even though we would still be friends our broadcasting relationship was over.

He did try to cajole me into going back to work with him, but I politely turned him down. 'I'll gladly help you in any way I can, but I won't be writing any more scripts, that's certain. If I ever write anything again I write it for myself, not for you.'

I feel Harry was jettisoned too soon by RTE. He should have had a programme long after he was pushed out the door.

I have fond memories of Harry. He was in his late eighties when he died, in April 2011, but in his heart he was going on twenty-three. I said at his funeral that I genuinely thought he would live for ever.

Our last conversation of any depth was at a luncheon arranged for reminiscing about the good old days in Henry Street with former colleagues who had worked on music programmes. We thought that maybe three or four would turn up for this trip down memory lane, but twenty-eight people, including Brendan Balfe and Mike Murphy, arrived for the lunch. We had it on the Barge on the Canal in late 2010.

We reminisced about the time I ripped up the scripts when we had the big falling out. 'Ah, yeah, you were a bold boy that day,' he said.

Harry was seriously ill for only a short time before he died, but he had been ill for a long time before that with other complaints. It was upsetting to see him in such bad condition, because Harry was always on the upbeat—always. If he was a musician he would be a jazz man: he wouldn't sing sentimental country songs like me.

He lived in Greystones and was in a nursing-home down

there. I can't really remember our last conversation when I went to see him, as it was quite upsetting, and he was filling up with tears. His wife, Frankie McDermott, a wonderful singer, asked me if I would say a few words at his funeral, which I was delighted to do—if you can call it being 'delighted' to speak at somebody's funeral. I told some of the funny stories about things that happened between us, like the betting anecdote. I had them laughing in the aisles that day. I dearly miss him.

Chapter 5 ∾

FREEDOM TO DO WHAT I LIKE

If I was starting all over again I would try to be less apprehensive about my situation as a freelance contractor with RTE. I was more or less living from year to year and would find myself going back in and nervously asking, 'So, what about next year?' And I would be told, 'Sure don't you know you'll be on next year! We couldn't go on without you.' I would walk away thinking to myself, 'Stop being silly. If the show you're working on is going to be on, you'll be on. They can't do without their best people.' But I had a real fear, even when I had fully established myself as a prominent broadcaster, of being let go.

I'd often think, 'Do I want to be on the staff? No, I don't. I want the freedom to do what I like.' I don't regret that. I'm happy enough with what I've done now that I am if not past the autumn of my career at least reaching the autumn. I'm by no means finished yet.

I am my own worst critic too. I know myself whether my work is good or not good. I always listen to stuff I do with a keen ear or eye on it and ask myself, 'Was that all right?' I don't want to boast, but I genuinely believe that I have done some of my best work in recent years.

It probably wasn't until the Jacob's Awards in 1972, when I was given the Sports Commentator of the Year Award in the radio category, that I felt confident that I was in the broadcasting game for the long haul. By that time I had been working steadily at RTE (as it now was) for sixteen years, but deep down I always feared that the work could dry up one day—particularly as I always had to hustle in those early days by coming up with the concept of the shows and then finding sponsors for them. So winning the Jacob's Award, which back then was one of the biggest things in the broadcasting business, was a huge deal for me.

I wasn't nervous on the night the show was televised live, because I had already been tipped off that I was going to win for my show, which was called 'Sports Line'. The trophy itself was a lovely solid piece of steel, rimmed with sound waves. It was one of the best and biggest awards I have received during a career that has spanned more than fifty-five years, making me one of the longest-serving sports commentators in the world.

Another reason that the night stands out in my mind is that the post-awards celebration may have been one of the last times I touched alcohol.

I gave up drinking for good on Ash Wednesday, 1973. My three daughters asked me to bring them down to the church to get their ashes. I brought them down and let them out of the car. I was sitting there and—though I'm the next-best thing to a heathen—I thought, 'I might go in and get ashes myself.'

As the priest placed the ashes on my forehead I told myself, 'I won't drink now until Easter Sunday.' But I began to enjoy not suffering from hangovers so much that I decided to give it up permanently. It was one of the best decisions I ever made.

I don't want to give the impression that I'm now anti-drink. Far from it; and I don't mind being around friends when they're enjoying a few drinks.

I gave up boozing because, to be completely honest, I was hitting the bottle too hard. I don't think it appeared to others that I might have a problem, but I knew it was becoming a serious issue because I was wasting too much time, and money, in the pubs. Besides, I didn't want my young children to see their father as a heavy drinker. We never spoke about it, but I think Marie was pleased with my decision also.

I never drank at home, but I was spending a lot of time in pubs with colleagues after we'd finished work. It's very hard in this business to just have the proverbial 'one'.

It wasn't affecting my work. I never went on air with any drink on me; I would have been afraid to, as I needed to be in total control. And I wouldn't have allowed anyone else to either, if I had been the producer.

But I did find it hard to give up the drink socially, because my colleagues wouldn't believe that I was sworn off it. 'Don't be codding us, Jimmy! Sure have one anyway. Sure that'll last for a week.'

I got through that with tons of stubbornness, and I just kept telling myself, 'I know I'll never have a drink again.' I had also given up smoking in 1971, because I had angina and the doctor told me that down the road cigarettes would kill me.

———

If the Jacob's Award was the highlight of 1972, the low point was being in Munich for the Olympic Games and witnessing the massacre of eleven Israeli athletic heroes by the Palestinian terrorist organisation called Black September.

I had been excited at finally going to cover an actual

Olympics for the first time, as I had been disappointed not to get to Mexico four years previously, in 1968. The first two weeks of the Munich Olympics had been wonderful, with an almost carnival-like atmosphere. The Germans were thrilled to be hosting the event for the first time since the infamous Berlin Games in 1936. There was a real sense that a successful Olympics would go some way towards erasing the militaristic image of wartime Germany, which was etched in people's minds thanks to the image, which always sent shivers down my spine, of Hitler at the Olympic Games, using them for his own evil propaganda purposes.

I know that the documentary *One Day in September* claims that security was lax in Munich, but at the time colleagues were remarking about it being the first time we in the media were aware of serious security at such events. Even getting in through the gate of the stadium was unbelievably hard, so tight was the security—to such an extent that my producers decided that I should do a piece for television depicting all this for the viewers at home. 'We want you to show how difficult it is to break the system.'

'Great. I'm looking forward to being your guinea pig,' I moaned.

The plan was simple: I was to attempt to gain entry to the Olympic Village without any identification and, I hoped, be refused entry. At Munich—as with any other city staging the Olympics—there was photographic accreditation, but in Munich you also needed a special pass if you were going to be at the news conferences, which allowed you access for three hours approximately.

Outside the village the cameraman concealed himself and the camera. We began with me speaking to the camera and showing them my special day pass for the village. I put it into my pocket, and then I showed my accreditation, without which I shouldn't be there at all, and then I took that off. Now, naked of badges, I strolled up to the gate to walk past security, but was immediately stopped—as we had hoped—and told I couldn't enter.

'I left my accreditation and pass back in the office,' I said, and then gave the security guard my accreditation number, which I knew by heart. 'You could check it with the powers that be. I have to get in urgently to do a piece on the Irish team.'

'Nobody can go through without a pass.'

I then spoke to him with the little bit of Irish I knew, and I baffled him so much that he got fed up and eventually told me, 'Go on inside.'

I felt that the whole piece, which had been sensitively and sensibly set up, was now a waste of time, because we had wanted him to refuse me entry. Little did we realise that my piece about breaching security was soon to become a sensation and to be beamed around the globe; for that night the Black September group broke into the athletes' village through the very gate that I had gone through earlier. We were inundated with requests for the film after other media heard we had it. I felt sorry for the security guard and would imagine he got into serious trouble over the incident.

It wasn't until the next morning that I became aware that terrorists had stormed the village. I had come into work early, and I remember thinking, 'There's an awful lot of action around the place.' Then someone said to me, 'Did you not hear about it during the night, that there were some Israelis killed?'

We had a ringside seat for the unfolding horrifying events, as just across the way from our office you could see the men in the white hats and the balaclavas on them. I looked up and saw police coming down the roofs. There were all sorts of eejits in the media camp who had obtuse ideas along the lines of 'Let's rush them!' This nonsense was coming from the type of fellow who couldn't even rush to the bar.

On the night when they began murdering the athletes I had been out for a drink in a little bar in the Olympic Park with the late Noel Andrews, and we heard a helicopter overhead. 'That's the boys being taken away to the airport. They got their wish,' I said, obviously thinking that the terrorists' demands were being met and hopefully now the Israelis would be released unharmed. But, tragically, it was when they arrived at the airport that the massacre took place. It was a horrific episode, which made me begin to lose faith in human nature.

Flowers are still placed daily at the site of the Israeli compound in the athletic village. The name of the street is Connollystrasse, after James B. Connolly, the first Olympic gold medallist of the modern games in 1896. I have been back there a couple of times and it never fails to send shivers down my spine when I think about those evil actions.

———

I have a nice story about Jack Nicklaus, who is still the King of Golf. He has won more majors than anyone else; the only one likely to catch him is Tiger Woods, who has fourteen titles, compared with Jack's eighteen.

At the British Open in St Andrews in 1970 I introduced myself to Nicklaus and asked him if I could interview him for Irish radio the next day, and he said that would suit. We arranged to meet outside the clubhouse in St Andrews at 1:30 p.m. As luck would have it, in the meantime the RTE newsroom rang me to ask me to do a news piece the next day at the same time. I thought, 'This will be awkward, having to go and find Nicklaus and tell him I had a bit of a problem with meeting him and explain it all.'

But he was very kind about it, telling me, 'Sorry about that, but we'll do it again.'

He was true to his word. Three years later, at the 1973 Ryder Cup in Muirfield, I spotted Nicklaus practising putting on the green. I went over to him and said hello and he replied, 'Hello! How are you? Would you like to do that interview now?'

Three years later and he still remembered. I thought that is the measure of the man.

We did the interview in the Muirfield clubhouse, which you cannot get into unless you are a member. The members are very honourable people: Major This or Captain That—no ordinary people! It was all very pretentious. But Jack brought me in, and we did the interview in the locker room.

On the day that I finally interviewed Nicklaus I went out onto the course while practice was going on; back then, journalists were still allowed to walk around the side of the fairway. Nicklaus was playing with Lee Trevino, Billy Casper and Arnold Palmer. 'Jaysus! Talk about Hall of Fame material!' I said to the others with me.

This demonstrates how talented these guys really were. During the tournament Lee Trevino, who was a great comic as well as a great golfer, was putting and doing a commentary to himself: 'Lovely putt from Trevino'—that sort of thing.

Somebody threw him a ball and asked, 'Can you putt that?' The ball was still in its wrapper, and instead of taking it off he putted it with the wrapper still on. He took it out of the hole, unwrapped it, and asked the man who threw it if he wanted it signed. He autographed it, put the wrapper back on, and gave it back to him.

As my colleagues and I walked up towards these living legends on the course, Nicklaus was slightly to the right of the fairway. He looked over to where I was and said, 'Hello, Jimmy,' and the others with me said, 'How do you know Jack Nicklaus?' I told them a little lie. 'Ah, sure we've been mates a long time.' I didn't tell them that it was only ten minutes after I interviewed him, because it wouldn't have sounded as impressive.

Tiger Woods, as I say, is probably the only golfer at the moment who can catch up with Nicklaus's impressive record. I met Woods in the most unusual circumstances in the year he won the Masters for the first time in 1997. He was only twenty, and already he had smashed the course record with fantastic golf, the likes of which had never been seen before.

There were hundreds of journalists waiting for him outside the press tent. I went outside and I noticed that there was a woman waiting there, who turned out to be his mother. We got talking about what a marvellous man he was and what a fantastic career he had ahead of him. Eventually Tiger came out to meet his mother. She said, 'Eldrick'—which is his real name—'I want you to meet my friend from Ireland. This is Jimmy. He's been keeping me company all afternoon' (though we were only talking for about half an hour).

Afterwards, at a press conference, I asked Tiger a question. He replied, 'And here's the man who kept my mother company!'

———

Soon after my memorable interview with Jack Nicklaus, I was very excited when I heard about 'Superstars', an American invention for television, launched in 1973, that had international stars from different sports meeting in competition in sports other than their own special field. Ireland became involved in it through RTE, and I was selected as the show's presenter for every season that it ran until NBC, the channel producing it, dropped it in 1994 because of a decline in ratings.

The first Irish winner was the great Kerry footballer Pat Spillane, and his prize was a visit to the World Superstars in the Bahamas. Over there Pat, who was a truly great footballer, competed well but didn't win.

One day Spillane and I watched some of the other athletes killing time by passing around an American ball to each other. Spillane was fascinated by this. He knew quite a bit about the American game. Toying with them, he said, 'You know these fellas who come out to take the kicks: how high do they have to kick it? How long do they have to kick it for it to be a success?'

They explained to him: 'It would have to be hit long, but it would also have to be high enough to stay so that the players could get up around it and not be off-side.'

He asked how long it would have to be hit for that to happen. 'If I hit it up to that boundary fence, would that be long?'

'Oh, Paddy, that would be fantastic.'

And then he asked in mock innocence, 'How high would I have to hit it? Would I have to hit it up to that cloud there?'

'Yep.'

He asked for a ball.

'But there's one difference,' they told him. 'When the ball is snapped back from the scrimmage there's ten thousand tons of flesh coming on top of you.'

They all got involved—even the truck-drivers and the television crew—and somebody snapped the ball back to Pat and, as everyone charged towards him, he kicked it high. Now

Pat was a fantastic kicker and a high kicker. He kicked that ball right up to Heaven's door and right down to the perimeter fence. They couldn't believe it, and they kept telling others and kept asking him to show it again. Sure Pat could do it with his eyes closed.

Pat actually got two offers to go to American football at that time, one from a New Mexico team and the other from a team in Ohio. They were telling everyone about the Irish footballer who could kick the ball so long and so high.

I was walking across the fields in Clones one day and a slightly irate Tyrone supporter came up to me and said, 'Sure what does Pat Spillane know about Gaelic football?'

'I don't know,' I shrugged and added, 'all I know is, Pat Spillane has eight all-Ireland medals and nine All-Stars. Apart from that, I don't know what he knows about it all.'

'Message taken,' he responded.

On one occasion, after the Superstars finished shooting, on our way back to Ireland we decided to stop in Mumbai (then known as Bombay). The producer insisted that we take a bus to the hotel. Of course I said, 'We couldn't go on a bus. We'll get a taxi.'

'No, you'll be ripped off in a taxi.'

'But sure what if they did rip us off? What would the actual charge be? You could quadruple the cost and still what would it be between a few of us!'

He kept insisting, and eventually myself and Marie, who was with me on the trip, got on this bus, which was packed like a tin of sardines. It was like one of those buses in the films that are full of people with ducks and hens and with suitcases stacked high up on the roof. The bus was jammed, and people wanting to get off at a stop had to be passed through the windows in this Indian heat. I kid you not.

We eventually arrived at this hotel that I had booked, the Taj Mahal Intercontinental. It had liveried porters outside. It was a beautiful hotel, one of the finest in the world, and we arrived as guests getting out of this clapped-out bus. I've never seen anything like it, with fellows getting onto the roof to get our cases down. Marie giggled about that bus journey and we staying in such an expensive hotel.

I didn't realise it until I began working on my memoir, but I was fortunate that Marie was able to travel with me to so many places. She was in such far-flung places as the Philippines, Australia, Hungary, Canada, New Zealand and America with me. These travels were mostly when our children were grown up, because when they were younger she was unable to get away from home.

On one of our trips to America in the early 1970s we visited Dallas, because she had always wanted to go there and do one of those tours where they bring you out to the ranches. I imagine this fascination was derived from watching the eponymous television show, which was the biggest thing on television at the time—apart from sport, obviously.

We stayed in the Fairmont Hotel, which is a beautiful place. A chap named Frank Zito got talking to us in the foyer, telling us that he ran the hotel's PR. I would later learn that this was a man who wore many other hats. It turned out that he was a friend of Jack Ruby's—or so he claimed. He spoke with enthusiasm when describing the night that Ruby murdered Lee Oswald. His story about the connection sounded believable enough.

When we mentioned that Las Vegas was our next port of call he told us, 'Everyone knows Frank Z in Las Vegas. So just tell them I sent you and they'll look after you.'

'Great. Thanks,' we responded, not sure about this boast.

In Las Vegas we decided to test it. We walked up to the Riviera Hotel, where Neil Sedaka was playing that night, and said to the door staff, 'Frank Z sent us from the Fairmont in Dallas.'

'Ah, Frank Z! How is he? Good old Frank! Big friend of Jack Ruby's, you know!'

And we were ushered in and given complimentary tickets for the Sedaka show.

I later learnt that Zito was one of the most infamous mobsters, who controlled criminal activities in the state of Illinois for more than twenty years. It so happened that this is where Ruby was from. Zito was charm personified when we met him, and you would never for a moment have thought that here was a crime boss who had worked his way up the criminal ladder after starting off as a bootlegger during prohibition before making his way into the seedy rackets of prostitution and illegal gambling.

I never met him again, as he died shortly after our meeting in 1974. But it just shows you who you can meet and what can happen when you travel all around the world.

——

About two years later, after my trip with Pat Spillane to the Bahamas, I was back at the Superstars and met Gerd Müller, who had scored ten goals in the 1970 World Cup and then four more in the 1974 World Cup, thus becoming the highest scorer of goals in the history of the World Cup until recently, when Ronaldo scored fifteen.

As we were waiting for the camera crew to set up we played five-a-side football and I got to see this German legend up close on the play. Now, not many fellows can say they have done that, calling passes from him and passes to him. He spoke only German, but we were able to communicate, because a ball is a bloody ball.

Another famous man who competed in the Superstars was Ed Moses, the greatest 400-metre hurdler in history. He held the world record for donkeys' years. He had competed in the Superstars show a few years earlier, and we had got to know one another then, because I was with him for about four or five days on set and we would do little one-to-one interviews.

During the Olympic Games in Los Angeles in 1984 I was outside the gates of the Coliseum one day waiting for the traffic lights to change so as to walk across, and right there beside me was Ed Moses.

As we stood at the traffic lights a car pulled up in front of us in which there were three or four Irishmen, who called out to me. Amazingly, I noticed that inside the car was Bob Tisdall, who had won the 400-metre hurdles in 1932 and on the same track as the man beside me, Ed Moses! There wouldn't have been more than three yards between the car and where Ed Moses was standing. In that space were the only two men who had won the same event in the same stadium, in 1932 and 1984. The Olympic Games in both years were held on the same track in the Coliseum in Los Angeles, the only time this has ever happened.

Being there waiting at the traffic lights was one of those moments when you wish you had a camera. And I wish now I had had the good sense to say to Ed Moses, 'Here's a special man I want you to meet,' and stop the car. It was just too awkward, because the lights changed quickly and the car had to move on. Neither of them knew the other was there—a historic moment for a sports buff like me.

The tragic events of Munich were still fresh in everybody's minds when only two years later West Germany staged the 1974 World Cup. Even though I had been to the 1966 World Cup in England, this was the first World Cup that I was sent to cover for RTE. I had been bitterly disappointed when RTE told us they had no budget to send anybody over to cover the 1970 World Cup in Mexico. It was painful doing all the commentary for the games in the studio, knowing that I was missing out on witnessing at first hand one of the most exciting World Cups in living memory.

Ever since I had watched my first World Cup, back in 1958 on an old grainy television, I had vowed that before I died I would go to the World Cup and would become a permanent World Cup-ite. Germany was the first of my twelve (so far) World Cups to cover.

The World Cup in Germany was truly a special occasion, and the highlight for me was seeing Johan Cruyff and the Netherlands play. I was commentator for the final itself. Who will ever forget the Germany v. Netherlands final, when the Dutch got a penalty within the first minute without a German having touched the ball! And that's no exaggeration: the first German to touch the ball was their goalkeeper, Sepp Maier, who bent over and took it out of the back of the net. The English ref, Jack Taylor, was a brave man making such a decision against the host country in the final.

I later met Johan Cruyff when, as secretary-general of the European Commentators' Association, I presented him with a prize as our player of the year at a match in the Anderlecht ground in Brussels. I had this beautiful trophy to present to him, which he knew he was going to get; but when I suddenly saw Pelé in the stadium I thought to myself, 'How could I present this trophy when the king is here?' Pelé, who I always thought was a football genius as a player and as a thinker of the game, readily agreed to make the presentation. Thankfully, I managed to get into the photograph with these two legends.

This was in fact the second time I got to meet Pelé, having previously met him in Germany at the World Cup. He was doing promotional work for Pepsi at the time, and part of this was allocating twenty-minute interviews with the great man himself, and luckily I got on the list. Anyway, our interview ended up going to forty-five minutes, because we were both so interested in talking about football.

I asked him how he got the nickname. 'Was it a flower? A small animal?'

'There is no meaning to it. It meant nothing. And as a child I hated the name and used to get into fights at school when other boys called me "Pelé" because I thought it was derogatory.'

I told him I had an idea about how he may have got the name. 'There was an Irish missionary priest in Brazil, near Santos, where you were raised. You were playing with a cloth or paper ball, because your family were poor, and you were fantastic with it, and the priest saw you. Now this was an Irish-speaking priest, and he said, "Féach an buachaill ag imirt peile," and all the oul-ones were around and going "Ahh! Pelé! Pelé!" And when the priest was gone the name stuck.

'Now isn't that a credible story?' And he agreed it was as credible as any of the other stories he heard. In his autobiography later he included a section on the Irish priest!

When I met him in Brussels to make the presentation to Johan Cruyff, Pelé asked me, laughing, 'How's my Irish priest's friend?' People began to believe this story, and that's how it began: I am the source of it.

Over time we became sort of half mates. I interviewed him one night in the Burlington Hotel in Dublin. We were sitting in the lobby beforehand and I said, 'There's a name you should know.'

'No, I wouldn't know any of the names of bars.'

So I brought him back to when he won his first World Cup for Brazil as a seventeen-year-old in Stockholm in 1958. I asked him who his captain was that day. The captain was Bellini, which is the name of the bar in the Burlington. He laughed. As I said to him, 'I'm full of useless information.'

I have only ever asked two people for autographs: Pelé and Maradona. I'm sorry I never asked for more, because I would have a great collection by now!

I was once on a plane flying from Mexico to Los Angeles and I was in the same compartment as Pelé. He slept most of the time but he woke up as the plane was coming into Los Angeles, and then these three Italians asked him for his autograph; they had a ticket or something from the World Cup in 1970 and they got him to sign it. He knew my face, so I went over and introduced myself.

'Have you ever asked for an autograph?'

'No,' he said, 'but there was one I would like; but it wasn't a footballer.'

He went all shy and wouldn't tell me who it was, so I didn't press him. I told him that I was the same, that I never ask for autographs. 'But I'm going to ask you.'

'Of course,' he said, and he signed a piece of paper for me. I thought this was the best thing ever, and I brought the autograph with me everywhere. When I changed suits I'd make sure to put it also into another pocket. I didn't want to lose it.

At the 1994 World Cup in America I met Maradona and I

thought to myself, 'I have to get his autograph.' I went up to him and took out the piece of paper with Pelé's autograph on it and asked him if he would mind signing it. He recognised Pelé's name, but he didn't say anything. So I have Pelé and Maradona on the same piece of paper; but unfortunately I can't find this precious piece of paper now! I hope one day I'll stumble across it again when I finally get around to doing some spring-cleaning.

But I'm not a great man for tidying up. I haven't even been able to find the home phone for the best part of a year now because I left it somewhere and the battery eventually died, and now I can't even ring it to find it!

Chapter 6

THE JIMMY MAGEE
ALL-STARS

My idea of putting together a charity match with famous sports stars was only meant to be a one-off, but somehow it got transformed into the Jimmy Magee All-Stars and it's still going strong. It has raised more than €6 million for various charities, which is a lot of money from a truly voluntary action.

When the All-Stars began people said, 'It won't last a week.' They were right: it has lasted forty-five years, which is a remarkable achievement for any charity. The All-Stars hasn't really stopped, as we still do one or two concerts a year to keep us together, but the football side of it stopped about five years ago, because, sadly, time crept up and we're all too bloody old to be running around a pitch; though I reckon that some of the older players who have retired would like to be still playing.

It all started when, during my days working alongside Harry Thuillier on 'Junior Sports Magazine', the two of us used to talk about organising a charity match. Then in 1966 I was chatting to an RTE producer, Bill O'Donovan, and we began talking about the idea.

'It's a pity we haven't got a team and have a kick-around,' I said to Bill.

He suggested that I should do something about it. I decided to explore the idea further. A great friend, Connie Lynch—who later went on to manage the likes of the Royal Showband, the Big 8, Brendan Bowyer, Pat Lynch and the Airchords—said to me, 'I'll happily organise it if you put the team together.'

I was excited at the prospect of putting together a list of who's who from sport, with some show-business people thrown into the mix. Nobody would refuse once I said it was for charity, so I was able to put together a dream team with the idea of giving punters an exciting exhibition match. I even had a picture in my head of the kind of jerseys we would wear: an all-white strip, like Real Madrid. In retrospect it was a ridiculous colour to choose, because all it did was show how out of shape we all were; perhaps I should have picked black instead, which can make you look slimmer!

The plan was simple. We always did a concert on stage after the show. We would play the match first, which I called the trailer, and then later they would come back and go to the gig.

For our first game and gig we headed off to Ballyjamesduff, Co. Cavan, on 6 June 1966. I didn't think of it at the time, that our first gig was going to be on all the sixes—6/6/66—but it wasn't a bad omen.

I had also organised the opposition team, which was mostly made up of two showbands, the Mighty Avons and the Drifters. It's no exaggeration to say that it was a huge success, and afterwards at the function in the parochial hall they were all coming up to me and saying, 'It's an awful pity that this is just a one-off, Jimmy. We'd love to do it again.' I hadn't dared to tell them the truth, that I already had a complete season of seventeen more games lined up, because I first wanted to see if it would work out.

'Actually we're playing next week in Tullow, Co. Carlow, and

Connie Lynch, Mike Murphy, Nobby Stiles, T. J. Byrne, Shay Brennan (RIP), myself and Alex Stepney in Dublin after Manchester United won the European Cup in 1968.

These glasses have come back into fashion; George Best liked them!

Jimmy Magee All-Stars at Croke Park in the early 1970s. *Back row (left to right):* Greg Hughes, Gene Stuart, Jimmy Swarbrigg, Maurice Reidy, Pat O'Donovan, Paul Magee, Ian Corrigan, Father Brian D'Arcy, Tom Hickey, Gerry Reynolds, Father Michael Cleary, Frank Murphy, Noel McCaul, Brian Harkin, Brendan Shine, Joe McCadden, Mick Leech, 'Gregory' and Seán Óg Ó Ceallacháin. *Front row:* Shay Healy, Dermot O'Brien, Steve Duggan, Peter Sheridan, Johnny Dawson (kneeling), Denis Ryan, myself with my son Mark on my knee, Frankie Byrne, Maureen Potter (kneeling), Gerry O'Byrne, Art Supple, Harry Ramsbottom and Connie Lynch.

Francina Blankers-Koen, 'Flying Fanny', the first woman athlete to win four Olympic gold medals, in 1948, chatting to me in her apartment in Amsterdam.

Racing commentary in Hong Kong.

Balance, eye on the ball, follow through—fitness oozing from every pore; where does this man fit in the all-time hot million!

Pelé, Paul van Himst of Belgium and Johan Cruyff wave to the crowd after the van Himst farewell match, 26 March 1975.

Myself and one of Ireland's greatest sportspeople, the cyclist Seán Kelly.

With the winner of the 1987 Tour de France, Stephen Roche, on the Nissan Tour.

When the Magees were together. *Back:* Mark, June, Paul (RIP). *Front:* Patricia, Marie (RIP), myself, Linda.

Left to right: The secretary of the Jimmy Magee All-Stars, Liam Campbell, myself, the singer Brendan Bowyer and showbiz manager Connie Lynch plan the All-Stars' visit to Las Vegas in 1989.

Larry Gogan, long-established icon of music on record.

the week after that we're in Parnell Park in Dublin, and the week after that we're in Roscommon.'

We soon went from playing local venues to playing in Croke Park in front of a large crowd, and playing in front of a massive crowd in Gaelic Park in New York. In 1971 we did a tour of America for the Cardinal Cushing Games and went to New York, Boston and Hartford, Connecticut.

The All-Stars was started at a time when the GAA sent official teams to America every year for the Cardinal Cushing charity. They went first to New York, then played Boston and then Hartford. One year there was a bit of a row between Croke Park and the Cardinal Cushing organisation and John Kerry O'Donnell, who ran the famous Gaelic Park in New York. The former champion hurler Seán Óg Ó Ceallacháin, who had a radio show on RTE on Sunday nights called 'Gaelic Sports Results', said to John Kerry that if 'real' teams were not going out he would get the All-Stars to go over and raise money. He persuaded us we should go out. We raised the largest amount the Cardinal Cushing organisation had ever raised by playing the three matches and three functions.

Sadly, he's dead now, so I can probably name Seán Purcell, who for my money was one of the greatest footballers in GAA history, in the following anecdote. On the first night of the tour he had one too many drinks after the flights. He wasn't the only one, but he was fairly well gone.

'Now, remember we have training in the morning,' I said, joking. These guys were jetlagged after our long journey and there's me telling them they had training in the park at nine o'clock the next morning.

Anyway Seán, who could hardly tell you his name at that stage, was the first man down the next morning in the lobby of the hotel. I said to myself, 'Now that shows discipline!' It was the discipline of top-level sportspeople who took me at my word and said, 'I must show by example.' This was about fifteen years after Seán was at his peak in 1956, but he still thought it worth his while, and that has always impressed me.

We've been fortunate with the calibre of people who got involved in the All-Stars at one time or another down through the years. I won't be able to mention them all, but the names that immediately jump to mind include Brendan Bowyer, Tom Dunphy, Dickie Rock, Larry Cunningham, Gene Stuart, the Indians, Doc Carroll, Dermot O'Brien, Jimmy Keaveney, Paddy Cullen, Seán Óg Ó Ceallacháin and Seán Doherty.

There was also Jack O'Shea, who was probably one of the four greatest Kerry midfield players in my opinion (the others being Paddy Kennedy, Mick O'Connell and Darragh Ó Sé). Paddy Kennedy played with me in the All-Stars and then refereed some games for us. Mick O'Connell was an honorary captain on a few occasions.

But one name that always jumps to my mind is that of the legendary Cork hurler Christy Ring. We were in Hartford one day and we were playing in a field outside the city, rather than a stadium. We were playing against a New York and Hartford selection. Before our game there was a softball game on, and the lads decided that Christy would be good at it and wanted him to have a go. Christy wasn't to be found, because he was away off at the far side of the field, hiding behind a tree but watching the game. One of the lads said, 'Sure he'll come over for you, Jimmy.'

I toddled over to Christy. 'The lads want you to have a go at this softball, Christy.'

'Do *you* want me to have a go at it?'

'Yes, Christy.'

'All right so.'

And we went back over.

'Give me that there what-do-you-call-it,' he said, knowing damn well what it's called. 'Is that a bat or a stick, or what do you call it?'

'A bat.'

'All right. Thank you. Now do you hold it like this or do you hold it like this?'

They were all questions he knew the answers to, because he had been watching the game.

Then he said, 'Now, who's your best pitcher?'

'Billy Kyle Junior.'

So, Christy asked them to bring Billy Kyle out. This young fellow of about nineteen came out and pitched for an underhand softball. Christy hit it and it went over the wall and down the motorway and kept going until it was out of sight.

'That's a home run now, isn't it?' Christy said. Then he dropped the bat and nonchalantly walked away.

That's the kind of man he was: he was only interested in perfection. Late in life he took up squash and became Munster champion though he had never played the game before. Very often he would ask you leading questions, such as, 'You were good on Saturday.'

'Thanks, Christy.'

'Who was the best player on the field?'

There's no definitive answer to that, is there, unless it's Ronaldo or Pelé! 'Well, I suppose, taking everything into account, Lindsay in defence.'

'You're a man who knows something about it,' he would reply, which meant that he agreed with me. Then he would go through the whole rigmarole of why that man was the best.

Christy was a winner all the way. He loved winning, and he knew how to win. He would say to you—we used a roll-on, roll-off system and I was playing on the field—'Did you find it yet, Jimmy?'

'What's that, Christy?'

'The thing you're looking for. You're running around the same spot, Jimmy. You haven't moved out of it.'

That was his way of getting at me because I was standing in the same spot.

'Did you lose your contact lenses?'

'No, Christy.'

'Well, let me out there and I'll have a look for you.'

So I would go off and he would come on. Jaysus, he went mad and scored a goal and a couple of points and then went back off again. You couldn't tire him out. At this time he was in his fifties.

Christy was a very, very special person. He died only eight years after this trip. He was a genius of a man.

After participating in the event for the Cardinal Cushing charity we decided to treat ourselves and we went to Las Vegas to do a show in the Gold Coast Hotel, which is just off the 'Strip'. We were to fly from New York to Las Vegas. As the plane ascended, Jody Sheridan, from Granard, Co. Longford, began to sing. He knew a lot of songs, so we asked him for 'The Gallant John Joe'. He finished just as we got into Las Vegas, having sung for six straight hours. I feel that really sums up the sort of thing the All-Stars was about.

On another flight the great trad fiddle-player Seán Maguire, and musicians such as Nita Norry and Dermot O'Brien, started a jam session when they discovered there was a piano bar on the plane. It ended up with the whole plane doing a conga up and down the aisle, with O'Brien and Maguire up front with the accordion and fiddle. This went on until we were flying into San Francisco and the pilot was telling us, 'I know it's terrific, I can hear it from here, but you'll have to take your seats, as we're coming in to land.'

We said, 'All right, we'll sit down,' but then suddenly they decided to belt out one more tune, and the pilot had to wait for us.

The stewards couldn't get over it all: they enjoyed watching all us Irish men dancing up and down the aisles. When we were getting off the plane they asked, 'When are you guys travelling home? Will you be travelling with American Airlines again?' It was obvious that they were hoping for a repeat performance. On the way back they had the red carpet rolled out for us and we were upgraded and given the full treatment. But we didn't dance in the aisles on the way back.

We always had a priest with us, and he would say Mass every morning. One morning Jimmy Keaveney, who played for St Vincent's and Dublin, was missing from the morning Mass in Father Brian D'Arcy's room, so they sent me off to look for him. I went around the hotel and when I found him I told him I'd been sent down to get him. He didn't really want to go back to the Mass but I persuaded him, and up he came back, huffing and blowing. During the Mass, Father D'Arcy would always ask if anyone had anything they would like to pray for or to say. Jimmy pipes up: 'I have something to say, father. I've never been to so many bleedin' Masses in me life. If I die this minute I'll go straight through the fuckin' roof, with clothes and all on!'

Everyone just laughed—including Father D'Arcy.

Before we got to Las Vegas we had arranged with the hotel that we could use the house band's musical equipment, because we hadn't brought ours with us, as nobody wanted to be lugging this stuff all over America. But what we didn't know was that the house band had another show that night; and when we were up on stage I noticed that, bit by bit, the equipment was disappearing. Then they came out and took the piano away. We looked at them and said, 'You can't do that!' Of course they replied that it was theirs, and they had to go to another gig.

We still had Mickey O'Neill—the Lord have mercy on him—on the drums; and then they took away the high hat, then they took the snare drum, and he was eventually left with nothing, just sitting on the stage with the two sticks. Then the fellow came up and took the two sticks out of his hand and left.

They continued to wheel stuff away in mid-performance, and then they began taking the guitars, and then the amps, and we were left with fellows on the stage with no instruments. 'Bloody hell! What do we do now?'

'Keep going—keep singing,' I urged them, because I could sense that the audience were on our side. But it has to be the first and only time I have seen a band disappear on stage.

———

I was coming back from an All-Stars match one night in the early hours of the morning, probably about three o'clock, in the car with Gerry O'Byrne, a former Kerry footballer, and Paddy Harrington, a Cork all-Ireland footballer who was also the father of one of Ireland's best golfers ever, Pádraig. The talk in the car turned to who was the fastest runner among us. They asked me, 'Are you fast?'

'Sure I would have been fast when I was young.'

'Would you be fast now?'

'I reckon I'd be faster than either of you two,' I said, cheekily.

They disagreed, and Harrington said, 'I don't know about that, Jimmy. I think I'd still give you a run for it.'

'You're on!'

'Wait until we get a stretch of road, and pull in and we'll do it,' says O'Byrne.

We pulled in on a stretch of road outside Monasterevin, Co. Kildare, and parked the car with the headlights left on to give us some light. We agreed that we would run from the car to the gates of Moore Abbey and back.

'Whoever wins is the Sprint Champion of the All-Stars,' I told them.

Could you imagine if anyone had seen three grown men up to this type of codology at three in the morning? Anyway, I won that battle, and I would have been disappointed if I hadn't, because I was the only sober one among us!

Harrington told his son about it, and at the Masters in Augusta one year Pádraig said to me, 'I never knew you were a sprinter!'

'Don't tell me your father told you that story!'

Sadly, Paddy Harrington is no longer with us. He was a wonderful man.

| MY WORLD TOUR

I decided that if you're going to call yourself a real sports broadcaster you have to see the major world events in order to know what you're talking about. So I decided to go on my own world tour in 1977 to see up close many of the iconic stadiums around the globe.

Looking back, I don't know how Marie put up with me, because I didn't really ask her if she minded me being away for so long. I probably didn't ask just in case she did mind and objected to this dream trip of mine.

I kicked off my sojourn by going over to watch the Tour de France. A friend of mine who worked for a Belgian television station, BRT, happened to be a good mate of the former cyclist Fred de Bruyne, got me accredited and agreed to take me in his car around the tour. Fred was a classic rider and a winner himself. We met through the Olympics, where at night some of the press corps would go singing and dancing. The tour was going a few days when I joined up. It was fascinating to be there watching some of the greatest cyclists; and they didn't get any better than Eddy Merckx, who happened to be the first cyclist I met on the Tour de France.

The cyclists register every morning. On my first morning there Merckx came up to sign in and casually handed his bike to his compatriot Freddy and asked him to hold it. So the first bike I got to hold in the Tour de France was Eddy Merckx's, without planning it. He was then, and still is in my opinion, the greatest cyclist of all time. It was a great thrill to meet him, because I love cycling and have always loved Merckx, who in his career won the Tour de France five times, the Giro d'Italia five times and the world championship three times.

Years later, when I was doing a television show called 'Champions' in which I interviewed fifteen sports legends in their homes or at the site of their famous victories, I made a point of including Eddy. We went to his house, where he makes his famous bikes. It was amazing being inside the house, half of which is a bike factory.

After leaving the Tour de France I booked a flight for South Africa with Swissair. I stopped off for a golf tournament in Switzerland and then I went to Geneva to get the flight, and it happened that the world chess championship was going on there. So, I had two days at that event, which was an enjoyable couple of days but also a bit lonely, as I had no-one to talk to.

People thought it was a bit odd when I told them my next port of call was Dakar, the capital city of Sénégal, a place I had always wanted to see. Besides, I had managed to get a connection flight from there to Brazil at an attractive price.

It's strange arriving at 4 a.m. in a place you've never been before. I got a taxi to the hotel, and when I arrived there were two armed guards on the steps. They were asleep, and the receptionist was also asleep. An unusual welcome.

The next day I went to the offices of the Senegalese Football Association. When I walked up the steps to the landing at the very top there was a huge photograph. You might expect it to be the president of Sénégal, or the president of the football association—but no, it was a photo of Pelé! I thought, 'Isn't that marvellous?' It shows how Pelé had transcended the mere mortals and the workings of other places. I then got a flight to Rio de Janeiro. I would love to be there for the next World Cup, in 2014.

I'm probably the only Irishman to have given a live commentary on Brazilian television. A friend of mine, named Walter, was a commentator for TV Global in Brazil, and I went to visit him when he was covering a game between Corinthians and Vasco da Gama at the famous Maracanã stadium. Half way through the game he turned to me and said nonchalantly, 'I have to go to the bathroom, my friend. Why don't you cover for me?'

'Sure I didn't know any Portuguese!'

'My friend, you don't need to know any Portuguese. You know all the players, and all you have to do is name the players.'

And with that he got up and left me with the microphone. 'Bloody hell,' I thought. 'What do I do?' I was afraid, but at the same time I was also half hoping there would be a goal scored so I could shout 'Goooooooaaaaal!' and mimic the way the South American commentators scream when the ball is slotted into the onion sack. I did about five minutes of this, just saying the players' names, with the occasional Spanish word thrown in, like *bueno* or *muy bueno*—even though I was in a Portuguese-speaking country. Later I was told that the fellows listening to it in the outside broadcasting truck thought it was great. Thankfully, nobody made a complaint to the station, but I'd imagine that my Irish accent, not to mention my Spanish, must have caused consternation to viewers, who were probably scratching their heads and wondering what the hell was going on.

When I was in the studio with Walter the same day he said to me, 'There is somebody I want you to meet. There is a very special man who wants to say hello to you, Jimmy.' He pressed a button, and there was Pelé on the screen, saying in a recorded video message: 'Jimmy, you are welcome to Brazil.' Years later Pelé would tell me that he remembered recording that lovely welcome message for me.

On this trip I also watched the great Brazilian player Garrincha playing football on the beach at Copacabana.

After my visit to Rio as part of my own personal world tour I went on to São Paulo, which is the largest city not only in Brazil but in the entire southern hemisphere, to watch some more games. There I came across a street football game called *futsal,* which today is popular everywhere but at the time I hadn't heard of it. At 12:30 the city centre would come to a standstill as they would mark the pitch and bring out the posts and sidebars right in the middle of the city. The excited crowds would gather for football played with a smaller ball and with fantastic skill.

Interestingly, when I came home I would wax lyrical about witnessing this, but people I would tell about it would say, 'It will never spread.' But it has, and I wouldn't be surprised if it was a game in future Olympics.

I know everybody praises Irish fans for being among the best in the world, but we pale in comparison with the carnival atmosphere that the Brazilians put on. And one particular Irish fan clearly knew this too. I was in Guadalajara in Mexico for the 1986 World Cup on the day that Pat Jennings played his last game for Northern Ireland to earn his 119th international, against Brazil. This Brazilian commentator had asked me if I would do an interview with him on the day of the match at an appointed time. Brazil always has a gang with them, dozens of people who dance and bang drums—and as many women as men among the fans. We started the interview, even though I didn't know any Portuguese, but he interpreted it there and then while the fans danced behind us the whole way through it. I don't know how I managed to keep my concentration during it all.

At the end of it a fellow broke from the crowd and came over to me. He said, 'Jaysus, Jimmy! I didn't know you knew Brazilian!' It was a fellow from Co. Clare who went to the World Cup and decided that the best gang to be with for the fun was the Brazilians. So he got a yellow Brazilian shirt with the number 10 on it and went everywhere with them.

For the record, Brazil beat Northern Ireland 3-0 on the day. I think Northern Ireland's best result was the quarter-final in 1958, or the magnificent result against Spain in 1982.

After São Paulo I went to Buenos Aires. I decided to go to a football match and came across a certain up-and-coming sixteen-year-old Argentine footballer. Argentina Juniors were playing Vélez Sársfield. At half time a sub came on. He was a little tubby for a young guy, with bushy kind of hair; but he was just sensational. I said to myself, 'This fella is unbelievable; he can do anything.' I knew even then that this kid was going to be an international sensation.

They don't have programmes at matches like they do here. I think this is based on the principle that all the home supporters know their own team, and they don't give a damn about the others. But there's a magazine there called *El Gráfico,* which is essentially a football magazine with some other sports thrown in. It had this feature of giving marks out of ten (which is now popular everywhere around the world), but they were very conservative, to such an extent that even if you played really well you would get a maximum of 7 out of 10, the average being about 6. Everybody seemed to get a 5 or 6 unless they were exceptional.

That night, after seeing Maradona in the flesh, I waited at

Avenida Florida, where the latest editions of magazines and newspapers would usually hit the news-stands at about midnight. I grabbed a copy of *El Gráfico,* which came out every week and after special matches. The ink was still damp. I looked up the match I had seen earlier, and there was the name Diego Armando Maradona. He played only half the match, and he scored 9 in the magazine. I thought to myself, 'This backs everything I thought when I saw him play.'

I'm open to correction, but I probably did the first piece on Maradona for a European publication when I wrote about him for my next column in the *Sunday World.* In it I said something along the lines of 'Watch out for this fellow in the World Cup, 1978. He is going to be the sensation.' Sure enough, a year later Maradona was in the Argentine squad. They thought he was too young to play in the World Cup, so, sadly, he didn't get any match time. Those who had heard me off air talking about him said, 'Ah, sure that was a lucky guess! Did you really see him play at all?'

'Mark my words,' I told them, 'you may have to wait another four years, but he will be there. He's the next great player.'

I was eventually proved right in 1982 when he arrived on the international scene and in 1986 when he single-handedly beat England with his 'different class', as I called it when commenting on that game.

I never had a proper conversation with Maradona, as he doesn't really speak English. I have talked to him, but through an interpreter, which is always unsatisfactory. But he knew that I liked him as a player. He was wonderful. Pelé and himself would be the big two players for me. I suppose George Best (who I will discuss later) would have been up there with them, but unfortunately he never played in a World Cup, and that wasn't his fault: how could he have played if the team isn't good enough to play in it? Nowadays there are two other great players that I admire: Lionel Messi, also from Argentina, and Cristiano Ronaldo of Portugal.

Reluctantly, after almost four weeks of a marvellous sojourn, it was time to return home. But my luck was still in when it came to meeting my sporting heroes. I had met Eddy Merckx, had been greeted by my personal hero Pelé, and had watched Maradona in one of his first games.

To cap a remarkable journey, when I was coming back to Europe from Buenos Aires I got word from a contact in Swissair that Juan Manuel Fangio, a Formula 1 driver who boasted a record of winning the world championship series five times, was travelling on the same flight as me back to Zürich.

I knew the seat he was in in first class (needless to say I wasn't travelling first class). When we were airborne I pressed the call button and gave the steward a note to pass to Fangio, asking him if I could interview him somewhere *en route* to Zürich. The steward returned and said, 'Señor Fangio would be delighted to, but he will do it after Rio.'

We touched down in Rio and were there for an hour. After we left Rio he sent a message down to me to join him at the front. I interviewed him in mid-air for about an hour. 'This is one of my great interviews,' I thought, 'talking to the fastest man in the world at the highest elevation I was ever at,' which was probably 33,000 feet. To this day he has the highest winning percentage in Formula 1—a remarkable feat when you consider how technology has dramatically improved since the days when he was behind the wheel. Even the great Michael Schumacher once said: 'Fangio is on a level much higher than I see myself. What he did stands alone, and what we have achieved is also unique. I have such respect for what he achieved. You can't take a personality like Fangio and compare him with what has happened today. There is not even the slightest comparison.'

I knew quite a bit about the man dubbed 'el Maestro' and 'el Chueco' (the bow-legged one), so that helped make it quite conversational. He was in his late sixties then but he was bright and fresh and still had a remarkable memory. He was still working for Mercedes and had the franchise for Argentina. He lived to the grand age of eighty-five and passed away in 1995.

———

The following year I returned to South America for the 1978 World Cup in Argentina. It was the second time that year I had been to Argentina, because I had also covered Ireland's participation in the hockey World Cup a few months earlier.

But the trip for the World Cup began on a worrying note when, as we were coming in to land in Buenos Aires, the pilot decided to abort his landing at the last moment and steer the plane back into the sky. While doing this he narrowly missed the control tower, and passengers sitting around me were as white as ghosts and some were screaming. For me it wasn't really a frightening experience, but it would have been if I fully realised what was going on. When I saw my fellow-passengers' reaction I told them, out of bravado, that there was nothing to worry about. The pilot had to make three attempts to land before touching down.

When I wasn't at games I would tag along with some of my colleagues to try the many wonderful restaurants in Buenos Aires. In fact the fellows had this thing about wanting to discover the best restaurant, and who had found it. To settle it all once and for all, four of us decided one night that we would have a dinner in Buenos Aires in five different restaurants. We had soup in one place, a starter in another, the main course in yet another, then desert in a fourth restaurant and coffee in a fifth. It was mad, but it was a sensational experience.

Of course it did help to have some perfect scenery—and I'm not talking about the landscape! For me Argentina can lay claim to having the most beautiful women in the world. The women between the ages of seventeen and twenty-four were just incredible. Yes, I was a happily married man, but I never felt it was a crime to admire such beauty.

The atmosphere at the matches was electric. Argentina were deserved winners of the tournament. They had some amazing players, such as Osvaldo 'Ossie' Ardiles, Mario Kempes, Daniel Passarella and Alberto Tarantini, who were managed by the chain-smoking César Menotti.

There were strange allegations about Peru throwing a match. I covered that match in Rosario. Before Argentina scored, Peru hit the post twice; so tell me how that could be a set-up. Argentina won, 6-0, and they had to win by four clear goals.

On the evening of the final, when they beat the Netherlands—who had also lost out in the previous World Cup at the last hurdle to Germany, after extra time—it was spectacular watching what appeared to be every fan in the stadium ripping up their tickets and throwing them high up in the air. I wouldn't have envied the cleaning staff in the stadium!

Afterwards I struggled back to my hotel. There was no transport, but no problems; there was bedlam, but no rowdiness. I circumnavigated the estimated two million people wildly celebrating on the streets as they sang 'Vamos, vamos, Argentina!' All the singing and shouting, noise, singing, noise, singing . . . it went on and on.

However, my favourite experience during that particular World Cup was a friendly game that was meant to be between the visiting press and the hotel staff but turned out to be something far more extravagant.

We used to play football wherever we were, so in Argentina we decided to get a game together, and we were wondering if we had enough players. As we were discussing this I noticed a very well-known person strolling into the hotel lobby, and I pointed him out. 'Look who's coming in the door. It's Bobby Charlton! Will I ask him to play?'

The others were aghast and told me, 'Jimmy, you couldn't embarrass us by asking him. He's a legend.'

I didn't let on that I knew Bobby quite well from covering football over the years, talking to him and doing interviews. I haven't seen him in an age now. I purposely never spoke to him about the Munich air crash in 1958, because I didn't know whether he would be comfortable talking about it. It's not a subject I'm too keen on myself. To this day it sends shivers down my spine when I reflect on one of the most inexplicable, eerie experiences of my life, when I did a radio interview with Matt Busby in his office at Old Trafford, and among the things we talked about was the terrible Munich crash of 1958. He lost a club really; he lost so many young men. I think that affected him a lot. He talked about all the great boys he lost, and went into a blow-by-blow account of what happened on the plane. When I was in the room there was as much quiet as there could be; the music was turned off altogether and nobody else was in the office except Busby, myself and the producer, Ian Corr. But when we listened to the tape there was an aircraft noise on it, which I thought was weird and eerie, because we weren't near an airport and there was no obvious sound at the time. There was this constant aircraft noise when we were talking about the plane crash. I do really think it was a sign. I didn't go into it too much because that sort of thing bothers me a bit.

Anyway, everybody that day in the hotel lobby was in awe of the great man, and all were impressed when he came over to me and said, 'Jim.'

I replied, 'Bobby, some of us here are lining up something.'

'What?'

'A game of football.'

'I'd love to play,' he said. 'I have my boots with me and all. What room are you in, Jimmy?'

I told him, and off he went. Ten minutes later the phone in my room rang. 'It's Bobby here. Listen, Jimmy, do you know who's in town as well? My brother Jack and Gento' (of Real Madrid). 'Can I bring them along to play too?'

I smiled and said, 'That would be great.'

Finally the match was arranged, and it eventually became European all-stars v. South American all-stars; but none of us press guys got near the pitch! I was supposed to be the captain, but sure that went out the window. The game was also meant to be played on a local pitch but was changed to a packed stadium after our team ended up including the likes of Bobby Charlton, Jack Charlton, Billy Wright, Ian St John and Denis Law, while South America had Labruna, Costa, García and the godlike figure of Alfredo di Stéfano, who played for Argentina, Colombia and Spain.

They reckoned di Stéfano was the greatest player who ever lived. He arrived on the day looking completely out of condition and had one of the biggest bellies I have seen on a human. When he came out that day there were 28,000 people there, and when his name was announced everyone stood up to acknowledge him with thunderous applause.

The level of skill displayed that day was fantastic. The game finished 5-3 to South America; all the goals were by di Stéfano.

I met Bobby a year later and he said he knew that day we

were playing against a different level of skill when it came to di Stéfano. 'To see di Stéfano and the size of him, and he was still able to put the ball over other players' shoulders.'

Chapter 8 ∾

COMEDY AND TRAGEDY

I once played a game of football in Red Square, in 1980 during the Moscow Olympics. If you haven't been there, let me tell you that you are immediately taken aback by it on first sight because of its vastness. At one end of it there is the famous St Basil's Cathedral and at the opposite end the State Historical Museum. Along one side is the Kremlin and the Lenin Mausoleum and on the other side there is the fantastic GUM department store, which sells everything from needles to anchors. And that is no exaggeration: they sell everything.

A gang of Irish media fellows were standing around waiting for Mícheál Ó Sé, who broadcasts for TG4 and Raidió na Gaeltachta, who was in the GUM. This Kerryman, who has played in half a dozen all-Ireland finals, came out clutching a ball he had just bought. It would be like bringing coals to Newcastle or curry to India: he buys a football in Moscow!

I convinced him to take it out of the wrapper so we could kick it around Red Square.

'You can't be doing that. You'll get us all bloody arrested,' one of the fellows was telling Ó Sé.

'Don't be silly. Get the ball out,' I replied.

But for a bit of devilment we put down our coats and bags

and had a three-a-side game. There was a military guard on duty in close proximity to us, and we wondered how we could get him into the game. None of us spoke any Russian, so I kept knocking the ball back towards this guy. He wouldn't budge when the ball hit him on the leg; there wasn't a move out of him, not even a blink of the eyes.

The lads were saying to me, 'Stop, Jimmy. We'll be arrested.'

We kicked it about a bit more and then I knocked it back to him, but he just ignored us, which was great discipline on his part. Finally, after about my fourth effort, he kicked the ball back to us and gave me a sly smile.

We laughed, and I said, 'Great stuff! We've beaten the system.'

And then the soldier laughed along with us.

I think Ó Sé can safely lay claim to being the only all-Ireland medal-holder to play football in Red Square.

We stayed in a hotel called the Cosmos on the outskirts of Moscow, just across the road from the famous park where they have the space shuttles on exhibition. In order to get into your room, when you got to your floor you were handed your room key by a woman.

Every day in the hotel the food was the same fare: a buffet breakfast and a buffet lunch. Three of the most common things were caviare, smoked salmon and steaks—unlimited amounts. After the first few experiments with this big spread we would end up discussing what colour caviare we wanted. 'Was the black better than the red, or was the golden one all right?' It was great grub, but it eventually became so monotonous that one of the fellows began craving just a rasher and egg.

When we were coming back one day from a press conference one of our guys, Michael Johnson, had this big book of about four hundred pages in Russian and he was wondering what he would do with it. So, on the journey back to the hotel he kept shoving it down between the seat and frame on the underground until finally you couldn't see it.

Later that evening we were going out to the Bolshoi and we left the hotel, which had unbelievable security. If you went outside the door you were examined, and if you forgot something and had to go back inside and out again you were examined. When we got outside there was this man waiting, who we had never seen before. He approached Michael and handed him back the book. 'You left it behind on the train.'

There was a story told that there were a few guys from Dublin going over to Moscow who were inundated with warnings about how the KGB would be spying on them and that everywhere they went it would be bugged. So these men began to become paranoid. They were in their hotel room, which was a big family room, but they weren't satisfied with it. So, believing there were bugs in the room, they began talking to the taps in the bathroom. 'I know you're there!' Talking to the knobs on the doors: 'I know you're there. I know you're listening.'

They then found the 'bug' on the floor, underneath the carpet. They went out and got a pair of steel scissors and cut the bug off. All that happened was that the chandelier fell down on the floor below! Sure there was no bug at all: it was the light-fitting!

On a previous trip to Moscow, in 1973, when Ireland were playing against the Soviet Union, there were a lot of Irish punters on the trip, and our guide was warning us to be very careful about changing currency, which at that time was two rubles to a pound, and that it was illegal to change it anywhere but in the official bureau.

When we arrived at the Hotel Ukraine I said to Liam Tuohy and a couple of others, 'Will we throw our bags into the rooms and go for a walk?' I was walking up the corridor from my room and I heard a fellow whistling at me—just like P. J. Gallagher in 'Naked Camera'—and it was your man, the tour guide. He had a great Brooklyn accent, and told me he could get me six rubles for a pound! 'Tell all the guys.'

I didn't know whether this was a trap or not, but I said I would pass the word around. A lot of the guys flocked to him. But when we got back on the bus he was just as strict about everything. I realised then about the two sides of Russia.

———

I was once barred from a pub; and it's all Eoin Hand's fault! It happened during the 1982 World Cup in Spain, when Northern Ireland memorably beat the hosts 1-0 in Valencia, thanks to a goal by Gerry Armstrong, who was a Gaelic footballer from the Falls Road.

I used to meet Eoin in a bar called Nagresco in Madrid. One night Eoin and some other revellers got me to sing a nonsensical song that I used to do, a bit like sean-nós, and eventually the owner asked me to leave because of it. I was barred—and I was the only sober one there!

On that trip Eoin rang up the English manager, Ron Greenwood, from my room one day. I couldn't hear Greenwood but I could hear Eoin, who was sitting beside me. 'Ron, Eoin Hand here, just ringing on behalf of all the lads and the people of Ireland, wishing you the best of luck tonight . . . And one other thing I just thought of, Ron: any chance of getting a couple of tickets to the game tonight?'

It's hard to believe that the manager of the Irish team hadn't got a ticket for the match.

Ron must have said he would do what he could. The deal was that when the bus arrived at the stadium for the England v. Spain game the driver would open the door ever so slightly, and Ron would quickly put out his arm and Eoin would grab the two tickets. That's precisely what happened; and that's how Hand got his tickets.

Later Michael Robinson, who we discovered had an Irish connection, was playing on the Irish team under Eoin Hand, who told him: 'If you really want to be a true Irishman you have to learn some of these old Irish songs. Have a listen to Jimmy singing them.'

Robinson comes over to me and I start singing my 'sean-nós' to him, which was basically me mumbling and every now and then singing the words 'factory wall'. He listened attentively and then later reported back to Hand. 'I can't understand anything,' he moaned. 'All I can hear is mumbling and then him saying the bloody "factory wall" over and over again!' Unfortunately for Robinson, Eoin told him that's what he would have to learn and sing, word for word.

———

When people ask me about Alex Higgins I always recount this anecdote, which sums up the personality of a man best described as a troubled genius, who tragically put himself into an early grave with his alcoholism and cancer. It was, if memory serves, before the 1982/83 season—the year in which Higgins would win his second world title—when I was invited over to do a piece for RTE television on a new snooker tournament called the Professional Players' Tournament, to be hosted in Birmingham and sponsored by Jameson Whiskey.

The filming was going great until it came the time to do a piece on Higgins, who, in his typical fashion, had disappeared out of the venue.

'Look, Alex is not here,' I said to the producer. 'We need him for this piece.'

'Will he be back?' he asked me, worried.

'Sure how do I know if he'll be back?'

We decided to hang on and wait. An hour passed. By this time it was almost 1 a.m. and we were exhausted from the evening's filming and were thinking about only one thing: going back to our hotel and climbing into our beds.

Eventually, the Hurricane stumbled into the hall.

'Quick, he's here! Go and ask him,' I said, nudging the producer.

'No, you ask.'

I went over to Higgins and asked him.

'An interview? Course I'll do an interview,' he said, his breath reeking of booze and cigarettes, though thankfully he didn't seem to be drunk. I had often seen Alex when he was in a messy drunken state, but I always stayed away from him, because he could be extraordinarily rude when inebriated.

Then he paused and, looking me up and down, said, 'You're Jimmy, right?'

'Yeah. And you're Alex,' I replied sardonically, as if he wasn't sure whether I was in fact Jimmy Magee, despite having met me on countless occasions.

'I'll do it on one condition.'

'Go on,' I replied with a sigh, sensing that 'here comes trouble.'

'I'll do it if you ask me two questions. You can ask me others as well, but I want you to ask me these two questions.'

I agreed. We quickly started recording and I began with his

two questions, which had sounded innocent enough but, knowing Alex, I was sure there was some hidden agenda at work.

'So, Alex, have you ever been to Ireland on your holidays?'

'Oh, I'm glad you asked me that, because the last time I was in Ireland I stayed in this place in Killarney, and it was a kip.'

And he went on about it and I thought, 'Well, that one is not bloody usable.'

After he stopped his rant about Killarney—which is far from being a 'kip'—I took a deep breath and asked him the second question. 'Alex, do you still play snooker exhibitions?'

'Oh, I'm glad you asked me that. I played for this fella and I told him I'd mention him on the air if ever I got a chance. So now I'm mentioning you, Jimmy. And I want you to know that cheque has bounced. And it has bounced again and again. So, would you ever send me my money?'

As he continued his rant about not getting paid for that exhibition I felt like throwing down the microphone and walking away.

'Now,' he finally said to me, 'that will frighten him.'

He then allowed me to ask some of my own questions. It goes without saying that we never had any intention of using his ranting episode in the finished segment. However, about six months later I was at Goff's, and I was upstairs walking around when I spotted Higgins coming towards me. I thought to myself, 'Here comes trouble! He'll be complaining that I never aired that rubbish he wanted in the interview.'

'Leave it there!' he said to me. 'By gee, I frightened that guy. I got my money. When he heard it on air he sent me my money rather than be embarrassed any more. So I wanted to say thank you to you, Jimmy.'

Another Northerner who was also a genius and sadly also

drowned himself in a sea of alcohol was George Best. I first got to know him well after I went over to do a feature on the Irish players in the Manchester United squad back in the early seventies. The feature was for the *Sunday World*, which I began writing for in its very early days. I had my first column in the paper in April 1973 and I have never missed a week—not even the week Marie passed away.

Best had made an arrangement to meet me for an interview at his famous boutique, but everybody was telling me not to hold my breath waiting for him to show up. I went to his shop about five minutes before our arranged time, and bang on time George strolled in. He was terrific to me that day.

About five years before he died I did a three-man tour of Ireland with him and Denis Law, who absolutely loved George and was always very good to him. He would never let anyone say a bad word about his former team-mate, or let anyone say a cruel word to George's face. I was the MC of the show, and these two great footballers would reminisce about their playing careers before we would open it to questions from the floor.

George was supposedly off the drink at the time, but every morning I would come in and he would have a snipe of champagne or wine in front of him.

'I thought you were off it.'

'I am! I'm only having the one to start off the day.'

I was worried that he was going to start hitting the bottle with a vengeance and we would have to start cancelling dates on this tour, which would be a crying shame for the genuine fans looking forward to meeting their idol. But, fair play to him, he stuck it out for the whole week on the road. He was great value for the punters' money, speaking up well and never once failing to give the audience a great show.

But—and there was always a 'but' when it came to George—

on the last night of the tour, out in the Spawell Hotel in Templeogue, he was ossified. He was so bad that he could barely mumble, and I was afraid he was going to fall off his chair on the stage.

I couldn't let him open his mouth on that stage, for fear of ridicule, because he was liable to say anything, something like 'Who the fuck are yeh lookin' at?'

Thinking quickly, I introduced the two to the audience and then I gave the security guy a nod that said, 'Get up here and take him off the stage.'

I then spoke to the audience. 'You're all here tonight to see Denis Law. You have to put up with me as the MC. And, of course, Denis won't mind if I say you're here to see your hero, George Best. If you know about football you know about George's life, and if you know about George's life you know what I am going to tell you now.'

I paused and looked around anxiously, taking a deep breath before continuing. 'In football very often the best players have little niggles and knocks and have to have fitness tests before big matches. Well, George has failed the fitness test for this match this evening, and he wouldn't be doing himself or you justice if he came on and tried to play. So we're letting him go off now, and I hope you understand.'

I held my breath as I waited for the fans' reaction. I could have been lynched by an irate mob, or they could justifiably have sought a refund, but as soon as I finished speaking there was a standing ovation as the security guards gently led George off the stage. Both Denis and I had lumps in our throats. I have never seen the likes of it, such love for the man and acceptance of his predicament.

The show was great; Denis was fantastic. I became George and myself rolled into one as I recounted stories about him.

Afterwards George said, 'I just want to say thanks to you. It was very nice what you did for me.'

'I would do it for anyone.'

It was only a few short years later, in 2005, that I did the commentary on his funeral for RTE. It saddens me to think that George, who was always in bloody trouble, could be still alive today if he hadn't continued to drink after getting a new liver. He was magical, a terrific player, but he was a total mess with his non-stop boozing. He was also good company, but I also saw him when he would not have been good company at all. A wasted talent.

Chapter 9

THE LUCK OF THE IRISH

I attended the world amateur boxing championship in Reno, Nevada, and then managed to grab a flight to Mexico a week before the World Cup kicked off in 1986. The plan was to have a few days off to relax but, as we all know, the best-laid plans can unravel. I became very ill soon after I arrived in Mexico, and I was so bad that one day I struggled down to the reception and pleaded with them to get me a doctor. It turned out that I was suffering from altitude sickness. The doctor gave me some medicine and, thankfully, it was all over in a day or two and I was ready for the World Cup.

When the rest of the boys arrived they all looked knackered, and they were asking me how I looked so refreshed. I just told them it was because of my good health. I wasn't going to tell them I was there a week and had only recovered from an illness.

I never saw any of the dangerous side of Mexico. The place was jammed with people and they were all lovely. It was a spectacular final, and a great one for Maradona.

I had to hop back and forth between Mexico and Los Angeles at the time in order to cover the Barry McGuigan fight in June 1986. On the flight back from Mexico I was on the outside aisle seat, and sitting beside me was a boy of about five with his mother. He was so disruptive, he was pulling lights and seats, and she just let him away with it, whereas I wouldn't have tolerated such behaviour. But I didn't want to say anything and start a row and then have to sit in awkward silence for the remainder of a long enough flight.

Eventually she went to the toilet. I said to the child, 'If you touch anything else on the plane I'll have you! I'm warning you nicely now, young man!'

I was sure he would complain about my threat to his mother when she came back, but he didn't say a word! He even kept quiet for the rest of the journey—not a move out of him. When we got to Los Angeles she said to me, 'Wasn't he good today?'

'He couldn't have been better.'

I'm sure the boy was relieved to see the back of me when I got off the plane.

——

While waiting for the boxing match I had a bit of fun in Las Vegas about Johnny Peters, who is on the cabaret circuit. For fun I would ask someone working in any restaurant or hotel I was in, 'Excuse me, has Johnny Peters been in today?'

And the reply was always 'No.' Sure they wouldn't know who Johnny Peters was! A few nights later I got a taxi and I asked the driver, 'What's the latest and biggest show on in Las Vegas at the moment?'

'I don't know, but all the guys are talking about Johnny Peters. He's the talk of the Strip!'

This whole thing emanated from me asking a whole lot of people if they had seen Johnny Peters. It just goes to prove that the Americans will buy into anything!

I was looking forward to meeting Barry McGuigan. I had been very friendly with his father, Pat, in his singing days. He was a fantastic jazz singer and he will always be remembered for his Eurovision days. Pat was mad for boxing, and I will always remember the day he told me about his young son at home 'who's a great puncher.' At the time I said to him, 'Sure all fathers are like that about their sons!' But he dismissed me and went on praising his son, who was about eight or nine at the time, and told me to 'mark his words,' his son would be a champion.

I first met Barry when I went out to his family home in Clones to visit Pat. The house would be filled with music, boxing, and quizzes to beat the band. They would be throwing out questions like, 'Who always jabbed with his left and crossed one-two to the body?' I was thrilled to watch from the sidelines as Pat's prediction about his boy began to come true.

When Barry won the world title in London in the QPR stadium over Pedroza, which was only the second time he had been beaten in more than thirty fights, I was there for RTE radio. At the end of it I was wondering who had the rights to do interviews with the new champion. Then I decided that I didn't care who had the rights: I wanted to speak to the man of the moment, regardless of red tape.

I asked my producer, 'Is there much lead on the microphone?'

'What do you want a lead for?'

'I want to get into the ring.'

But the producer began protesting that we hadn't got the rights to do that.

'Sure what about all these American fights you see in the films, and they always get into the ring afterwards!' I said.

He insisted that he couldn't do it, because we didn't hold the rights.

'I'm going to get into the ring anyway,' I said.

He was right, of course, because the BBC had the rights in Europe and ABC had them for America. But I got into the ring anyway and made my way over to Barry. All the cameras were there as I got into the ring. I made eye contact with Barry, and he immediately began coming towards me across the ring and we met half way. 'Jaysus, Jimmy, we did it!'

They were the first words he spoke after winning the world title. And, yes, I cheekily got the interview.

Barry was always generous to me with his time, regardless of which television stations had the first rights to speak to him.

He was a fantastic boxer, but unfortunately he lost the featherweight title in Las Vegas to the relatively unknown Texan boxer Steve Cruz. There was something odd about that night. Firstly, the heat was horrendous. Those who know these things say it was 125 degrees Fahrenheit, but other reports say it was 110 degrees. Fountain pens were melting on the press table. At the end of every round servants would come around and put wet towels on the back of reporters' necks.

Barry was in the ring fighting not just with the lights for the television but also with the sun beating down in the middle of a boiling afternoon. He told me he doesn't remember anything from the tenth round on, but by the end of the fight he was out on his feet. He was knocked down twice in the last round, and only for that he would have won the title. I know this because I had befriended a woman who worked in the offices there and I went to her after the fight and asked if I could look at the score cards. One judge had McGuigan behind, another had him ahead, and another had him level with the relatively unknown Cruz. McGuigan, as the champion, would have got the advantage when it was that close, as was the norm; but getting knocked down twice in that round decided the one remaining judge, the one who mattered, to go for Cruz.

At the end of it all McGuigan passed out from dehydration, as he had had no water from the tenth round on. But he was apparently shouting, 'Don't let them close my eyes!' because he was afraid of death. This was because he had been in the ring with a lad who died after their match, Young Ali (the Nigerian Asymin Mustapha). That fight affected him for a long time. They found out afterwards that he had an aneurysm which would have erupted as soon as he hit something.

I only spoke briefly to McGuigan before the fight. He told me he had a sore ankle that he had hurt in training, but he wasn't making an issue out of it.

He stopped fighting soon after that loss, which resulted in a very costly legal row with his manager, Barney Eastwood. I got on very well with both men, so I was sorry to see that happening between them. Boxing is full of these sorts of stories, but everybody always thought that McGuigan and Eastwood would last the distance. You could say that, up until they quarrelled, it had been a match made in Heaven.

———

The following year at the 1987 Tour de France I had a pain in my leg, and someone said to me, half joking, 'There's a new laser wagon on the Tour.' This was a laser treatment that was still new at the time. I marched over to the wagon and asked them to look at my leg, and they looked it over. When I came out there were four cyclists waiting impatiently outside, and one of them was Seán Kelly. 'So you're the man who's holding us up! That's gas; we're riding in the Tour de France and Magee is in the tent!'

Kelly had a groin problem and had gone on a 25-mile spin

that morning to try to loosen himself up, but he couldn't do it, and he rode the rest of the Tour de France with that injury. The man is made of iron.

Now at after-dinner speeches he tells the story of how I held up the injured cyclists.

I would guess that I have been to the Tour de France about eight times. My biggest memories are of Irish riders, such as Kelly and Roche, when they were at their peak. Both were great riders; it's very difficult to say which one of them was better. Roche was a classic rider: he won the world championship, the Tour de France and the Giro d'Italia. Kelly won a lot of one-day classics: he won Milan–San Remo, Tour of Flanders—all the big ones. But I think the climbing held him back in the Tour de France; he was too big to be a climber.

I was very proud when the Tour de France came to Ireland. It was brilliant, but it has the anti-climax of being remembered as the year with all that trouble, when the Belgian team were caught with illegal substances. The man who won that year was the cheating Italian Marco Pantani. The pirate is dead now as a result of cocaine poisoning.

It would be hard to argue against naming Lance Armstrong as the greatest cyclist in the modern era. I first got to meet Lance in 1993 in Oslo, where I was covering the World Cycling Championships. The amateur race was on the Saturday and the pro race on Sunday. It was a dirty day, with heavy rain. I think the weather was so bad that every rider fell, including Kelly and Roche.

Armstrong was still in his teens at the time but he won the event, and the Americans went crazy. I met his mother and she was telling me, 'He is hoping to ride in the Tour de France and even win it.'

On that day you could see the potential in him. He didn't

appear to be egotistical but he was a driven man. He would be right up there with Merckx. But nobody could have imagined the rollercoaster journey he went on after that. I don't believe that his mother that day even dreamt he would go on to win the Tour de France an astonishing seven times—not only that but during it all to get cancer and then come back with a bang.

There were a lot of people saying he wasn't a fit man to represent the sport because they said he was on illegal substances. I think that any man who has suffered testicular cancer has to be on some form of medicine, so damn it, I would forgive him if he wanted to live.

———

There was this fellow named Grimes from Dublin who became famous for a while because he always sneaked into big events. He was first rumbled when he was brazenly walking a horse in the Grand National and an editor from the BBC turned to a sports reporter and asked, 'Who's that guy who's walking in the horse for the Grand National?'

'Same guy who walked it in last year.'

'What are you talking about?'

So they began investigating who he was, and it turned out that he had been gate-crashing all these events.

One night I was MCing at the Albert Hall in London and this guy in a dinner suit approached me and asked me, 'Do you know who I am?'

'I do, actually. Sure I saw you on the BBC when you breached all security.'

'With respect to you, Jimmy, I'm going to go out on the Albert Hall stage. I've never done it before, and I'm going to do it tonight. The hall is packed.'

'It's very nice of you to tell me, but I don't think you should do that.'

'I'm telling you because I don't want you to think I'm being a smart arse here.'

'Stay there. I have a better idea,' I said to him, as I was informed it was time for me to kick off the show. I walked onto the stage to introduce Brendan Shine and his Band. 'And just before we greet Brendan Shine,' I told the audience, 'I have a little bonus for you. Do you remember the man who walked the horse in at the Derby? Well, he's here, appearing at the Albert Hall for the first time.'

I brought him out so he didn't have to break the security, and he got a massive reception. It just shows that the Irish are magical for fellows like this character who break the system.

He was very grateful for it. 'I never thought I would be introduced onto a stage.'

He asked where we were going next. I told him the Lincoln Centre in New York.

'I'd love to go there.'

But I told him that I didn't think the security there would let him on stage. If he did go over, alas, he wasn't able to breach security that time, because we never met again.

———

Also in 1987 I began doing a television show with George Hamilton called 'Know Your Sport'—a title I had come up with. We were sitting around one day thinking what we might call this sports programme. The idea was already there, and George was already involved, and then I came in with the title.

I also wrote all the questions.

The show was a great success, and the first prize was a trip to the Olympic Games in Seoul in 1988. The first winner was a man called Tom Hunt from Waterford. His two nephews Stephen and Noel Hunt have played soccer for Ireland, and both are playing at the moment.

I didn't need to win the main prize to get over to the Olympics in Seoul, which was a lovely experience. The Koreans are a lovely people. There was an unfortunate woman who ran a stall in the open market in Seoul where they sell everything from needles to suits and shirts. This woman had no arms or legs and she would shuffle around on this piece of leather. She was quite speedy and efficient and getting the jobs done and looking after things. She was the voice of the place. One of the lads was looking at her, saying how unbelievable she was. I told them they should have been there the day before when the bus pulled up and the driver opened the door of the bus and said to the woman, 'How are you getting on?' Every time I meet Frank Whelan since then I say, 'How are you getting on?' But it's a private joke that only applies to those in the know about the woman in Seoul.

————

Before heading to Asia I spent the summer in West Germany covering Euro '88. I suppose the Irish soccer team had been the 'nearly men' up until they qualified the first time for a major tournament. Even though we had quality players and had enjoyed the occasional magnificent result over the years—such as laying claim to being the first international side outside the Home Countries to beat England on home soil, back in 1949—

we were overshadowed for far too long by our Northern counterparts when it came to qualifying for tournaments.

Before Jack Charlton took over as manager both John Giles and Eoin Hand had been desperately unlucky not to have succeeded in getting Ireland into the World Cup. There was certainly an abundance of the proverbial luck of the Irish with our qualification for the Euro '88 tournament. We got there only by the skin of our teeth, thanks to a late goal by Gary Mackay in Sofia that put Ireland top of the group and unceremoniously dumped Bulgaria out of contention.

Nobody had expected Scotland to beat the Bulgarian side, but it was a result that opened the doors to a desperately desired resurgence in the Irish soccer team, who were moments away from getting to the semi-final in Euro '88 and reached the lofty heights of the quarter-finals in Italia '90, as well as qualifying for two further World Cups, first in America and then in Japan and South Korea.

At long last Ireland was there on the major stage, which was very special. It was a hell of a good team too, with such wonderful players as Liam Brady, Ronnie Whelan, Mark Lawrenson, Frank Stapleton, Kevin Moran, Paul McGrath, Packie Bonner, Kevin Sheedy, John Aldridge—players who were performing with flair at the top level in English football. So it was a terrible shame that Jack Charlton went on with this mantra of 'put 'em under pressure,' which was even more prevalent in the Irish squads that played in the two subsequent World Cups under Charlton's charge.

I would have loved to see the Irish side go out and play positive football, as they did in parts of the game against the Soviet Union in Euro '88 or, to take another example much later, when an Irish team—and one that was lacking the creativity of the players under Charlton—outperformed the

French in Paris in 2010, which will also be remembered for Thierry Henry's infamous handball.

It was a shame that Jack had a notion in his head that they would play this 'put 'em under pressure' style of game. He told the players to go out there and 'put their backs under pressure, and don't let them have a free kick at the ball.' As it turned out, it worked considerably well for him, up to a point. It was a system that Greece, who were truly a brutal team, used to greater success when they ground out result after result to win the Euros in 2004.

If the Greeks could accomplish the unthinkable one can only imagine what that Irish team, with its abundance of talent, could have achieved with different tactics.

Apart from all the star names it was a squad that also included a young Niall Quinn, who was with Arsenal then and had got his first cap in 1986.

I was pronouncing his name with the Irish pronunciation, but one day the head of sport at RTE asked me, 'Where did you get "Kneel" from? His name is Niall' (pronouncing it 'Nile').

'I know that's what they call him over in England, but it's wrong.'

'I'm telling you, his name is Nile, not Kneel, and that's what he's to be called.'

So from there on I reluctantly called him Nile. One day I got a letter from Niall's mother, a short one-page letter saying, 'Only his father, myself and yourself, Jimmy, call my son by his proper name.' I didn't have the courage to go back in with the letter to RTE's head of sport and say, 'I told you so!'

Years later I was doing a Sunderland game and Quinn was playing that day, and he said in front of a lot of people, who were probably wondering what he was on about, 'I think we've lost the battle, Jimmy!' meaning his name.

I probably would have explained to the listeners about Quinn's name if I had got a chance to do the commentary on any of the Irish games in Euro '88, but sadly I didn't. I was thrilled to be there, but I was equally disappointed that the game roster—either by design or accident—meant I was not selected for any of the Irish matches. I felt it was unfair on me after years of loyal service not to be given at least one of our games. I knew all the Irish squad by their first names. Many of them approached me in Germany and to a man would ask the same question: 'Why weren't you covering the game? Were you sick, Jimmy?'

It saddened me, sitting alone in my hotel room watching them play against England when Ray Houghton headed in that famous goal, which he likes to sing about as his party piece. Houghton was a great player, and I still meet him regularly out in RTE. He was essentially a right-footed player, so it's funny the way life works out, as I think it's fair to say that he got two of Ireland's greatest goals ever, one with his left foot and one with his head, and neither of them with his favourite weapon: his right foot! It was the same with that other famous Irish goal against the Russians in Euro '88: Ronnie Whelan hit it in off his shin, as it turned out.

After Ray Houghton's score against England I kept telling myself, 'I want to be there at the game instead of this bloody awful way of watching it,' as I cheered on Ireland during the unbelievably tense game, when England missed chance after chance, thanks either to a fantastic Packie Bonner or to the posts and crossbar. Perhaps we were blessed by the Rosary beads that Packie kept in his gym bag.

After the final whistle went and we won 1-0, I was still fuming, and I decided to get the lift down to the hotel's restaurant for a bite to eat. As I sat there eating I told myself,

'You have to exorcise all that out of your head. You have a game tomorrow. You can't go around having nasty thoughts about anybody or anything. It's past tense—get on with your job.'

It did cross my mind that perhaps the powers that be felt I simply wasn't good enough to be trusted with big games. When the thought that it was a reflection on my work crossed my mind I told myself, 'Well, why I am doing any of them?' So clearly it wasn't about a decline in the quality of my work; but to this day I just don't know why I wasn't selected. I probably didn't fight enough for it; I might have questioned their decision but was brushed off with a simple 'Sure aren't you going to the championships—what more do you want?'

I managed to cast off the bitterness and enjoy the rest of the tournament. I was fortunate enough to cover the Netherlands, who had a top-class team with the likes of Marco van Basten, Ruud Gullit, Frank Rijkaard and Ronald Koeman. Ireland were desperately unlucky to lose 1-0 to the Netherlands with a goal in the dying minutes that was clearly off-side. Similarly in 1984 I was fortunate enough to cover the games of the French team, who were the ultimate winners.

The morning after the English game I was going to collect a rental car, which was across the square from the main cathedral in Cologne, when I noticed that there were four Irish guys on a bench looking the worse for wear. I was wondering to myself, 'What the hell are they doing here? The match was in Stuttgart yesterday! That's almost four hundred kilometres away!'

'Ah, the Memory Man!' one of them shouted in my direction.

'Ah, it's the Memory Man!' another piped up.

I was trying to walk fast, as I had a schedule to keep, but I also didn't want to be rude to my compatriots, so I went back to them.

'You're the Memory Man, right? You know everything, right?'

'I am indeed. What do you want to know?'

'Where's our bleedin' hotel?'

'You're in the wrong city, lads!'

I laughed along with them. They had got on the wrong tram after the match and then got on another tram and then decided to take a taxi and ended up 370 kilometres away.

Reflecting on it all, it's hard to believe that it took us a staggering twenty-four years from Euro '88 to qualify again for the Euros. But, unfortunately, we don't have the same quality of players today as we had in Jack Charlton's era.

Chapter 10 ∾

| DOUBLE TRAGEDY

After all these years I still become emotional when I think about 1989, undoubtedly the most difficult year of my life, when I lost both my wife and my mother within months of each other.

The year had begun on a real high when the 'Late Late Show' had a special edition to commemorate my broadcasting career. It was actually the first of two special shows the 'Late Late' did about me. The first one was a beautiful surprise, because I hadn't got the slightest idea about it when I walked onto the set to be warmly welcomed by Gay Byrne, a friend whom I've always had great admiration and respect for. I thought I had been invited on to do a piece about Ireland's two great cyclists, Seán Kelly and Stephen Roche, who had won the Tour de France only two years previously.

Marie, Lord have mercy on her, had obviously been a party to the whole ruse, but I genuinely never realised that a special show was being planned for me. I arrived in RTE that evening and said Hello to everyone in the lobby and then went up to get my make-up done. When I arrived in the make-up room Seán and Stephen were already there and chatting about cycling. As I greeted them, the floor manager rushed in and announced, 'There's a slight problem. Two of the guests are held up at the airport. Jimmy, is there any chance you would go on first?'

I shrugged and replied, 'I'll go on whenever you like.'

He then turned to Stephen and Seán and asked them if they were ready and said he would bring them down first and come back for me. When I eventually went downstairs Gay met me outside the door of the corridor.

'Ah, Jimmy. I'm so glad to have you here. It's very nice of you. I'm sorry to have to do this out of order.'

I replied that it wasn't a problem, and I walked into the studio with him and sat down. What I didn't know was that while Gay was chatting off stage the show had already been going out live. Apparently Gay opened the show by saying, 'Good evening and welcome. We have only done a few of these before'—which was true, as up till then they had done a special 'Late Late Show' only on Noel Purcell, Maureen Potter and the Chieftains—and he then said, 'We have another of those, a very special man, and now I'm going to go out and meet him. And he knows nothing about this.'

So he went off stage to get me, which he has never done before, and brought me in and sat me down. Sitting in the other seats were Father Michael Cleary, Barry McGuigan and Harry Thuillier.

We talked for a while, and then Gay announced, 'I think we should take a commercial break.'

It still hadn't dawned on me that the show was all about me until, during the break, my eyes wandered around the studio and I noticed Marie, Paul, Linda, June and Patricia. Even then I just thought, 'The cheeky so-and-sos never told me they had tickets for the "Late Late Show"!'—because I knew I hadn't got them tickets. Then I saw another few friends; and then I began to recognise more and more people.

When Gay came back to his seat I asked him, 'Is there anything going on here?'

'No. We'll let you go off in a few minutes, as we know you have another appointment.'

'Yes, I have an appointment, but it can wait.'

'Do you like to sing?'

'No, I can't sing.'

'Ah, come on.'

Reluctantly, I got up and sang a song—out of tune, of course. Then I sat down and said to Gay, 'Listen, is this all about me?'

'Have you not rumbled it by now?' he laughed.

The whole thing was about me! It was a fantastic honour. At the end of the show they brought out this cake and a clarinet, which was Marie's idea. Why a clarinet? I must have told her during our courtship that I wanted to play the clarinet, I wanted to be like Benny Goodman and I wanted to swing. This was my Dixieland instrument of choice, but I could never afford one when I was younger. There was one in the window of McCullough's music shop in Dawson Street, and it cost half a crown (12½p) a week, but I wouldn't have that much to spare, so I never got the clarinet. It was a wonderful gift. I still have it but, sadly, have not learnt to play it.

Several years later Pat Kenny did another special on me when he was the presenter of the 'Late Late Show'. And, believe it or not, that was another big surprise, because I never imagined they would consider doing a second special show about me. On that occasion I was supposed to be on to discuss motor neurone disease, which at the time had tragically been diagnosed in my son Paul. When I went onto the stage Paul was sitting front and centre in the audience.

When this book comes out perhaps Ryan Tubridy will do another one on me! I've actually been on the 'Late Late' with Ryan, so I have the great honour of having been on the show with all the hosts.

Soon afterwards tragedy struck when my mother passed away in New York. Looking back, I wish I was there more for my mother. She had a huge interest in travel; she loved visiting places and all that. I would have given anything—though financially at the time I couldn't afford to bring myself anywhere—to be able to walk into the kitchen as a young man and say to her, 'There's a round-the-world ticket and hotels and some spending money.' I would love to have been able to do that for her, but when I did have the opportunity to have enough money to do that she wasn't there any more, and that's a big regret.

My mother was about eighty when she became ill. She deteriorated quite rapidly in the closing stages, which was an awful pity. She really loved life and being around people, especially her children and grandchildren.

Near the end she was in and out of hospital in New York, and I flew over a few times to see her. I would normally visit her about twice a year, and I truly missed her when we were apart. I hadn't lived with her for a long time, and she had a new life, so in a way I had to get to know her again when she remarried, but at the same time she never really changed for me.

She used to come back to Ireland regularly to visit her grandchildren. She adored them all, but she had a particularly close bond with Paul. Perhaps it's because he was the oldest, but he was the one that was most likely to be with her. As a twelve-year-old he even went with one of those 'unaccompanied children' tags on a flight to New York to see her. She later told me that when she met him at the airport and asked him what he would like to do all he spoke about was wanting to go to a bowling alley; of course she didn't want to go to one, but he pestered her so much that she brought him, and he practised and practised, and only six years later he became an Irish champion. Eventually he became the manager and coach of the Irish national bowling team. He loved all sports and at school was cross-country champion, and he was a good Gaelic player; he even played in Croke Park and won a medal. He was also a very good golfer, and I believe if he had had more time to concentrate on it he could have been a professional; but then you can't do everything in this world.

I often think that if there's such a thing as reincarnation Paul will come back as a jockey. Reflecting on this, it's strange and terribly sad that they are both gone now.

When I realised my mother was very ill I dropped everything and headed over to see her. I think she knew she was dying. After our last conversation she asked when I was leaving, 'Ah, Jimmy, when will I see you again?'

There was nothing profound in our conversation, just everyday stuff. I think she wanted to keep the tone light rather than having a really heavy conversation like 'Look after yourself, don't be doing this,' etc.

I kissed her goodbye and told her I'd be back as soon as I could get away. Deep down I knew I would never see her again. I kept myself together until I got out of her apartment.

I don't know how I got through that time. I've got through a lot of stuff in my time now that I think about it. I would cry silently to myself, or cry loudly on my own, but you can't let everybody else down. People would be looking at me, saying, 'I wonder how Jimmy is?' and thinking, 'Well, Jimmy is just fine,' because I always stopped myself from breaking down in front of others.

When I left my mother's apartment I got a taxi and went back to the hotel to pick up my bags to go to the airport. As the

Jack Charlton tells me how it's got to be.

Conor O'Dwyer, Seán Boyle, Peter O'Neill, Gerard Cooke, myself and Tim O'Connor with Redundant Pal in the winner's enclosure at Leopardstown after winning the Ladbroke. (*Courtesy of Healy Racing Photography*)

Giacinto Facchetti, captain of the 1970 Italian World Cup team, and Bobby Charlton receive awards for their contribution to football at a ceremony in Rome in 1990.

Boxers Wayne McCullough (silver medal) and Michael Carruth (gold) renew memories of the 1992 Barcelona Olympics with the commentator.

Harry Thuillier, the man who gave me my first break and remained a favourite character.

Showing the red card at the 2000 Garda Sportstar Awards.

Myself and Olympic swimmer Michelle Smith de Bruin in 2003 launching my video *Greatest Sporting Memories*, the proceeds of which go to the 3Ts (Turning the Tide of Suicide), an organisation that creates awareness, research and education about suicide. (© *Ray McManus/Sportsfile*)

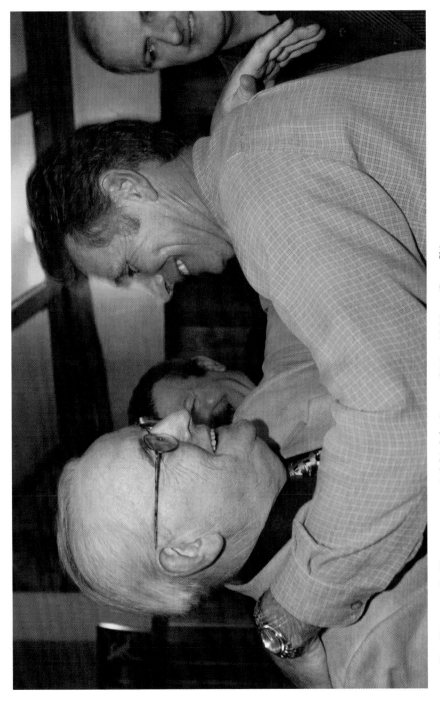

Myself and Eamonn Coghlan on my seventieth birthday in 2005. (© *Ray McManus/Sportsfile*)

2006: Mike Tyson trying to stare me into submission—or is he jealous that I had more hair than him? (© *Collins Photos*)

Myself, Mícheál Ó Muircheartaigh and Brian Carthy celebrating RTE Radio's eightieth year of GAA championship coverage in 2006. (© *Matt Browne/Sportsfile*)

Sporting Legends: Members of the 1956 Irish Olympics team honoured in 2006 by the Association of Sports Journalists in Ireland. *Back (left to right):* Peter Byrne (president of the ASJI), Dermot Sherlock (Olympic Council of Ireland), Ronnie Delany, Pat Sharkey, Rossa O'Reilly (son of the late Brendan O'Reilly), Harry Perry. *Centre:* Fred Tiedt Junior (son of the late Fred Tiedt), Freddie Gilroy, myself, Tony 'Socks' Byrne. *Front:* John Sommers Payne, Maeve Kyle, Niamh Kinsella (daughter of Eamon Kinsella), Jocelyn Emerson, Sandra Martina (daughter of Gerry Martina), Johnny Caldwell. (© *Brendan Moran/Sportsfile*)

cab pulled away I thought to myself, 'I will probably never see Mam again.'

She passed away about a week later. I knew the second I picked up the phone and heard the voice of my sister Mary at the other end that she was gone. It wasn't as big a surprise as it might have been for, say, people who are killed in accidents, but it doesn't lessen the blow nonetheless. Adhering to my mother's last wishes, they brought her body back home to be buried.

————

I was only coming to terms with losing my beloved mother when we were dealt another blow when Marie died suddenly the same year. She was only fifty-five. At the time she had a chest problem, from bloody smoking; apart from that she wasn't sick really. She lost a lot of weight and had been unwell for a bit but never really did very much about it. She was unwell in a typical Irish-mother way. You would ask her what was wrong and she would tell you, 'Nothing's wrong.' She was never off her feet, even when ill. I didn't notice that she had got so thin; it was only when it was too late that I noticed it.

I can't really remember my last conversation with Marie. It might have been one of those arguments about something—not a real argument, something like 'What are you wearing that suit for every day?'—the sort of trivial thing when I was leaving the house for work.

She went to bed that evening and she didn't wake up. I was going out early and I had been up half the night, because I had been in late, and I was getting a bag to head out again when I found her. It was a horrendous experience. I don't know how long she had been dead.

I ran into the next-door neighbour's house; I don't know why you would do that but you do in such moments of sheer panic. They rang for an ambulance, priest, and all that, and then I faced into the daunting task of telling our children that their beloved mother was dead. It was something that simply empties you of any emotion.

The funeral was a blur. It took me a very long time to get back to anywhere near normality after Marie's passing at such a young age. When I was a young teenager I had to become head of the house, and now when Marie died I had to become the minder of children again, though they weren't exactly young: the youngest, Mark, was nineteen, and we helped each other to get over it together.

It's now more than two decades ago; and when Mark left home I was on my own again, which can be lonely at times.

What kept me going at the time—and still now really—is the future. What am I going to be doing in the future? Where am I going to be? To be in London this year (2012) for the Olympics, or Brazil in 2014 for the World Cup? To be in Rio in 2016 for the next Olympic Games after London?

I moved on without any great plan after Marie died, but I had work commitments and I was determined to meet my obligations. If anything, it would distract me. However, I couldn't sleep well afterwards and it took me a while to sleep properly. I didn't cry as much as I should have, because I think it is good to cry. But I didn't. I didn't really cry when Paul died either. I cried inwardly, but I never cried in front of people, as I didn't want to make an exhibition of myself.

It did take time to get over waking up in the night and Marie not being there, or being welcomed home with a small row. 'Where were you until this time?' Funny things, or stupid things, like arriving in late and putting the key in gently and tiptoeing upstairs and then thinking, 'What am I worried about going easy for?' I can let chairs fall now without anyone hearing—that's a realisation. I never feared I would let myself go after she died, and I wouldn't do that, and I'm not going to do it now.

Marie was extraordinarily good to me. She did so much for me. I probably never really told her how much I appreciated her and how much I valued everything she did for me and our children. When you are mixed up in show business you are not home as much or as often as you should be. She always hung in there, no matter what happened. She encouraged me in those early days when I was doing loads of sponsored programmes and events, and things were looking up. I knew there was a long way to go but things were looking good, when all of a sudden all the programmes went off the air, from no fault of mine: sponsors' contracts had run out. I would be making less money and then even less again, but Marie never panicked too much or complained during those tough periods. She was extraordinarily good with me, and patient; she could have told me to go out there and get a 'proper' job, but she never said that.

When I think about her today I fondly remember how we travelled together. When the children had grown up she came with me to a lot of places when I was away working. We went to Asia, Australia, all over North America and all over Europe together. We were at the Niagara Falls in Canada, dressed in the yellow oilskins to stop the spray on your neck. We had good times together.

I suppose my fondest memory of Marie would be of the patience she had with me. There I was scooting around the place, and she would ask where I was going next. I kept reassuring her that next year I would be earning more money, and she would just say, 'Okay, I believe you.' Thankfully, it turned out that I was right. But she wasn't there to see the best days of it.

It's been more than two decades since she passed away, but I never got involved in another serious relationship. Life is like a ledger: there's a credit and a debit side. Ideally they should balance. Do they always balance? No, because occasionally I'm a lonely man. I was thirty-three years married to Marie. I think I have handled her loss well, but that doesn't mean that I don't miss her or get lonely.

Funny enough, I like living on my own now, but I don't want to be on my own all the time.

I still wear the Claddagh ring given to me by Marie on my ring finger. I also wear my father's wedding ring on the other hand, which would have been given to him in 1932. I have worn this since he passed away. I'm not a ring man, but I always wear those two. I used to take my father's ring off when I washed my hands but stopped doing this after I went away without it one night when I took it off in the toilets of the old Metropole in O'Connell Street. After I left the restaurant I suddenly realised I wasn't wearing it. I dashed back into the hotel and went downstairs and asked the attendant if he had a signet ring with the initials P.J.M. on it.

'You're lucky,' he said, 'because an honest man found it on the washstand and handed it in,' and he handed it back to me. It taught me a valuable lesson, and I've never taken it off from that day to this. I would take neither one of them off unless I truly had to.

I almost had the rings stolen from me when I was doing a signing session at Tallaght Town Square, around the time it had just opened. A rough-looking fellow came over and said, 'Give me something.'

I asked what I could give him. 'Give me something. Give me a ring!'

I told him, of course, that I wasn't giving him my ring, and even if I wanted to I couldn't take it off. He was telling me he would get it off for me when the security man came over to see if I was all right and asked what was going on, and he moved the fellow on. He then said to me: 'See that guy? I bet he wanted your ring.'

I said yes, and he told me he probably said he would 'take it off you.' And he added, 'Don't doubt him, because he's just out of jail. He took off a woman's wedding ring with a hacksaw.'

As I said, you meet some people!

Chapter 11

WORLD CUP AND OTHER TOURS

On a personal level, I was grateful to be going to Italy for the World Cup, because I hoped the trip might help to divert my mind from the pain I was feeling after losing my wife and my mother. At that point I was very low, and I couldn't see myself ever managing to recover from those huge losses. There isn't a single day that goes by without them entering my thoughts, but I have learnt to live with my fate. As the adage goes, time is a great healer. But I would probably have fallen into a million little pieces if there hadn't been a World Cup to motivate me to keep going.

I was there when Ireland qualified for the World Cup in Malta. The night was wonderful, because we were on the verge of achieving the unthinkable. I did the interview with Jack Charlton immediately afterwards on the field. Yes, he was ecstatic, but the euphoric Irish fans took him aback. He didn't know what was going on; he couldn't understand these mad Irish fans. (Those are my words, not Jack's, I hasten to add!) He could never understand why there were so many people on the streets of Dublin when the team came home after getting knocked out in the quarter-finals by Italy. His view was 'But we didn't win the thing!' And he was right: we didn't even win a match in the World Cup. We did beat Romania on penalties—in fact that match was a draw, but it has to be decided that one of the drawing teams can move on. Nobody ever says, 'It was the greatest game ever, with the best team ever.'

Again I have to say I was disappointed with the decision made by RTE before I went out to Italy that I wouldn't be doing the commentary on any of Ireland's group matches, against England, the Netherlands or Egypt. Theoretically I could get an Ireland game if they got to the quarter-final, to be played in Rome, and probably against Italy. It was an attractive prospect.

So, it was all planned out ahead what matches would be done, by whom and where and when—and all I could do was keep my fingers crossed that Ireland had a good run and got to Rome; otherwise I would have the dubious honour of being one of the world's longest-serving sports broadcasters who never did the commentary on his national team at an international tournament such as the Euro or World Cup.

I've often wondered why RTE decided not to use me, and the only reason I can think of is that a new man came in, George Hamilton—who I have great admiration for—and that he had stipulated in his contract that he would do the Irish matches. Maybe RTE thought it would be trendy to have a younger person doing the commentary for the Irish games, or maybe they just felt he was better than me—which is not up to me to say, but I personally don't think so.

The same thing occurred in 1994. I don't do a lot of Irish matches now, though I did a friendly against Slovakia recently. George obviously has a contract, and that's what we have to go along with. Although I'm friendly with George, I've never spoken to him about it or asked him. I've been told that's the way these things work. It's the same in the BBC, with John Motson appearing to have a monopoly on English matches.

But it was frustrating, and before I headed over to Italy I did approach the management in RTE to vent my views about it, but sure what's the point? Once it's a *fait accompli* there's no point in worrying about it any more. They didn't really give me a reason.

I never rocked the boat in RTE; I never really pushed myself into anything with them. Maybe I should have pushed myself; many people, including members of my family, have said to me, 'You're too soft! You're too soft!' And maybe I am. But what harm has it done me? Well, say I had done another hundred Irish games, would I be any better off today?

Before heading over to Italy I decided that I wasn't going to let it sour me or unduly worry me, as it had done with Euro '88. 'Just get on with what you're doing and be grateful that you're going,' I told myself as I boarded the plane.

But the football gods were smiling on me, and Ireland did get to the quarter-final in Rome against Italy. Finally my first Irish game was happening and, as it happens, it's still to this day the biggest game we ever played in.

I walked into the magnificent Stadio Olimpico with Liam Brady as the 73,000 fans crowded in. I could tell that Liam, who was loved by the Italians after his days with Juventus, Sampdoria and Internazionale, was disappointed that he wasn't going to be playing that night. He should have been playing, as he was only thirty-four and had officially retired only the previous month, after finishing his career at West Ham United. Instead he was there that night as an analyst.

We were walking up the ramp to the stadium, and these guys manning the gate suddenly saw Liam Brady and began shouting his name and running over to him in turns to shake his hands. I told him that it showed what they thought of him there still, because he hadn't played in Italy in a while and he hadn't ever played for a team in Rome.

He just said, 'It's nice.' I thought it was better than nice.

Unfortunately the game turned out to be far from nice for Ireland. It was a sad day really, because there was such a good feeling about the Irish team over there. I thought they might have done it that day. And they were only defeated by one goal in the thirty-eighth minute by Schillaci, who seemed to score at will in that tournament.

To begin with, he didn't even make the starting team: he came on as a sub in the first match and scored and went on to score in every other game he played in. In the 1988 European championships Marco van Basten, a great Dutch player, didn't get in the starting team either and came on as a sub and then retained his place and became the top scorer of the championships.

Schillaci did a lot for me without me having met him, because every time I was being turned away from a restaurant because it was too full I would say to the maître d', 'Ah, Schillaci! Mwah, mwah'!' And they would suddenly get the table for me. 'Schillaci' was the magic word.

Back home Ian Corr, an RTE producer, asked me to do an intimate interview piece with Jack Charlton, because we knew each other very well. He wanted me to talk to Charlton in the way a couple of friends would talk to each other about the World Cup and things that the rest of us mere mortals may not know. Jack agreed to do it, and we met in the Shelbourne Hotel for tea and cakes.

I began by saying, 'So, Jack, tell me this. Tell me something that you know that the rest of us don't know about the World Cup.'

'I'm glad you asked me that. We're playing Italy, and I've said to the fellas, "I want you to play it over the top." And Kevin

Sheedy says, "We don't do that at Everton; we play to feet." I told him, "I don't care what you do at Everton. This is not Everton, and don't give us that insubordination: play it over the top." Sheedy says, "But—" I said, "No buts at all, play it over the top. Get it?" Sheedy then says, "Do you mean if I have the ball I don't pass it to one of my own team?" "Correct."

'So what happens in the game—Sheedy has the ball. Aldridge is there and calls for it. Sheedy passes it to Aldridge and it bounces away from him. The Italians get it, run it down, cross, and it comes to your man Donadoni, and he has a shot. I ask Packie for one save. He can only parry it away, and that fellow Schillaci got the only goal. It was hard luck for Packie, bad control by Aldridge, but it wasn't their fault: it was Sheedy, who didn't do as he was told. Had he done what he was told they wouldn't have got the ball, and they wouldn't have got that goal.'

'Jesus, Jack, that simplifies it!' I replied.

I've always enjoyed interviewing sport personalities like Jack Charlton and getting their insider's view on major events.

———

About this time, in the late 1980s or early 90s, I was working on a television project called 'Champions', which had me go around the world to interview fifteen sports stars for a kind of 'where are they now?' programme in which they reflected on their achievements. Yes, I know, it's very nice work if you can get it. It was a fantastically produced show, commissioned by an independent television company run by Mike Murphy and Larry Masterson, who is a former producer of the 'Late Late Show'. It came about when the two of them were coming back from Australia and were discussing ideas on the flight. Their cameraman, Séamus Deasy, said, 'I've a great idea, but before I tell you what it is I want to emphasise that it belongs to Jimmy Magee, because he put it to me a long time ago. So I'll tell you all about it, but then I don't want anybody stealing it, because it's Jimmy's.'

He explained that the idea was to go to the places and talk to these people. Where are they now? What are they doing now? Are they still fit and healthy?

The boys thought it was a great idea, and they got on to me about it and said they would produce it and I'd present it.

We did it in bits. One of the first trips was to Australia, which turned out to be gruelling, because we had to get there and back quickly, as we were on such a tight budget. We jetted out on the Monday, arrived in Perth on Tuesday, went straight to work doing an interview all that day, then got the plane that night to Melbourne, and two days later back up to Sydney and then home on Friday on a night flight. We were wrecked; however, I'm that mad that I would gladly do it again.

We first went to Perth and interviewed Margaret Court, who was the queen of the tennis courts. She had made history by being the first woman during the Open era and the second woman in history, after Maureen Connolly, to win all four Grand Slam tournament singles titles in the same calendar year.

After that we went across to Melbourne to meet Herb Elliott, who was easily one of the greatest 1,500-metre runners in the world. In his time he was the best, and even now he would be well up there. He ran before the advent of those fancy tracks: he ran on grass and he ran on gravel, but he was stupendous. He was never beaten over a mile or 1,500 metres in any race, by anybody, anywhere. There were no world championships during his time but there were the Olympics, and he won the 1,500 metres at the 1960 Rome Olympics in a runaway. He came to Ireland in August 1958 and ran at Santry when Billy Morton brought him over *en route* from the then Empire Games in Cardiff. It was reckoned that Elliott was going to break the world mile record, which had first been broken in 1954, and set a new record time. In a wonderful race, which I was there to witness, Elliott won; the first five men were all inside four minutes. It was the greatest mile race up until then, and Elliott ran 3'54.5". The first man ever under 3'55" was Herb Elliott. His famous trainer was a man called Percy Cerutty, who trained him like a dog, like a slave.

We wanted Elliott to bring us to Portsea, out to the sand dunes where he trained with Cerutty. It would pull the legs off you running in sand dunes. Out he went with us—thirty years after his prime—and he got into his running singlet and shorts and running shoes so we could get pictures of him running on the sand. We told him that he didn't have to run, but he insisted so that it would be authentic. As I watched him running quickly across the sand I thought, 'There's not an extra pound on him after all these years since his retirement. He's mighty.' I'll never forget him, and how generous he was with both his time and his body.

When we had tidied up all our stuff he wanted to bring us out for a meal to his house, but reluctantly we had to turn down his kind offer because we had to go to Sydney to do another interview. In retrospect I think we should have taken him up on it after what happened next.

The crew got the bright idea of making a road trip. 'Wouldn't it be lovely to drive from Melbourne to Sydney?'

'Ah, would you come on and we'll get the plane. The plane is fast. It'll take us six or seven hours to drive.'

But they insisted, and I reluctantly gave in. Séamus was driving, and after we drove across the city of Melbourne I asked him if he wanted me to drive for a while. He said yes, so we switched over.

I drove for about thirty miles and then turned around to discover that the other three were sound asleep. These are the boys that wanted to see the bush and wanted to see Australia. Only one person was awake, the one who didn't want to drive: me!

I drove for another two hundred miles and then I said to them, 'That's enough of that. I'm pulling in for the night.'

We stayed in a place called Yaz. It was so remote that the fellow had to open the hotel when he saw us coming. To make matters worse it was the coldest and dampest place I've ever had the misfortune to stay overnight in—and, believe you me, I've been in some cold places. It was so bad in this hotel that— I'm not joking—we had to heat ourselves with the television! Picture this: the television would be turned on and put under the covers of the bed, and then we'd take the heat from the set—fully clothed. So that was our night in Yaz. Yes, Australia is a lovely place, always warm—like hell!

———

After this trip I went over to the Netherlands to meet Francina Blankers-Koen, known as 'Flying Fanny', who was the first woman to win four gold medals at the same Olympic Games. She went to the Olympics in 1936, little more than a child, to compete for the Netherlands on their relay team. She was to become the greatest athlete of all time, as we all thought. Sadly, the next Olympics were scheduled for 1940 but weren't held, because of the Second World War. The next ones after that, due in 1944, weren't held either. In 1948 Fanny was thirty and the mother of two children, but she still qualified for the Olympics in London and won gold medals in the 100 metres, 200 metres, 80 metres hurdles and 4 × 100 metre relay. That was a fantastic performance. This was my second opportunity to meet this incredible character. About fourteen years before the 'Champions' programme I had gone over to the Netherlands to do an interview with her for the *Sunday World*. I had made contact with her through her daughter, who worked for the Dutch television channel NOS.

When I visited her in her apartment in Amsterdam I asked her, 'Have you still got the medals? 'Yes, I have,' she replied, and she began pulling out drawers and bits of things and eventually produced the four medals. It was wonderful to hold them.

For 'Champions' we went out to her summer home on the picturesque canal banks. By now she was in her eighties, but she still wanted to swim for us to show us how fit she was. She was one of the most fascinating women I have ever met, a truly wonderful woman. I thought this woman would live for ever, but sadly she died in 2004. I will never forget Flying Fanny.

Our next big trip for the series was to the United States, where I met Peter Snell of New Zealand, who was a three-times Olympic winner; Mark Spitz, the swimmer; Floyd Patterson, the boxer; and Arthur Ashe, the tennis player, who tragically died from AIDS.

We headed for New Paltz, New York, to meet Floyd Patterson, who has the distinction of being the first fighter to regain the heavyweight championship of the world. There were no airs or graces about the man, who died in 2006. He opened the front door to us, and the first thing he said to me was, 'Did you ever hear of the Iron Man from Rhode?'

I smiled and said, Yes. Every Gaelic footballer reading this book will know of Paddy McCormack, who played for Rhode, Co. Offaly, and was known as the Iron Man from Rhode for good reason. One of the Heavey girls from that area married Floyd Patterson, and she must have told her husband about this somewhere along the way. It fascinated me to hear him being mentioned all those miles away from Rhode. We had a bit of a laugh about it.

We then went on to meet one of my absolute heroes, Arthur Ashe, at his home in New York state. We arrived in this little town where he lived. We found the right street but couldn't find the number of the house. There were two women out in their garden, so we asked them if they could help us find Arthur Ashe.

'Arthur Ashe? Miriam, do you know Arthur Ashe?'

'What does he do?' the other woman asked.

I told them he was a professional tennis player, a Wimbledon and American champion.

'Sorry, never heard of him,' they said dismissively.

I ask you, how could they not have heard of the first black man to win Wimbledon?

We were sure we were in the right place, but we thanked the women and went on. We walked up the next avenue and asked someone if we were in the right place to find Arthur Ashe. I was shocked to learn that he was living next door to the two women we had previously asked and who had professed no knowledge of him. Now, either they were totally ignorant of the fact, or ignorant of tennis, or just so plain ignorant and racist that they didn't want to recognise a black man.

I asked Arthur if he would pick up a tennis racket and hit a few balls for the camera. It was something we had got other people to do: Jackie Stewart drove a car (albeit a private car) and we got Eddy Merckx on his bike.

'I'll do anything else, but I can't play tennis,' he said, politely but firmly.

So we left it. I was puzzled, because he was so gentlemanly about everything else and showed us all his pictures and what they meant. He didn't cut anything short, but under no circumstances would he go out and play tennis.

I didn't learn until much later that he couldn't play tennis any more because of his illness with HIV, which he had contracted from a blood transfusion after a second heart operation in 1983. He simply hadn't the energy. He did look tired, but you wouldn't know by looking at him that he was so ill. He did say to me that he was very tired and 'had to take life easy.' It was only then that it began to dawn on me how bad he was.

Arthur Ashe was still only forty-nine when he died in 1993, which was not too long after our memorable meeting. When he died I cried. I was in Madison Square Garden in New York at a boxing match the night he died. In boxing, when someone has died they ring the bell ten times, which is known as the prayer for the departed. They did it that night, and an announcer came on and said, 'We'll take a little break now from this fist feast, because one of our greatest ever has passed away to his eternal rest. Ladies and gentlemen of Madison Square Garden, to the late Arthur Ashe.'

I was stunned. When I looked around at the boxing crowd getting to their feet in his honour, tears trickled down my face as I thought back to the time I had spent in his company.

———

The staging of the 1992 Olympics in Barcelona was one of the best ever. I happily remember walking down towards the old Bull Ring. You come to an incline that goes up towards the hill of Montjuïc and the Plaça d'Espanya and the water fountains. At night the fountains were all coloured, and the song 'Barcelona', written by Freddie Mercury and sung by the Catalan soprano Montserrat Caballé, would be floating out of the speakers and onto the packed streets. It was just hair-standing-on-end stuff.

My personal highlight of the Barcelona Games was when I was having my lunch one day in the hotel on my own and I noticed two women sitting near me, who happened to be the only other people in the restaurant. One of the women looked very familiar.

'I know you,' I said to her. 'I think you're a famous Olympic 100-metre champion.'

'Yes, but do you know my name?'

'I knew who you're not. You're not Rio Mathias! . . . You're Wilma Rudolph.'

'That's the one.'

It was a nice ice-breaker. We reflected on her life and times. She was one of seventeen children born to a sharecropper in Tennessee. She had polio until she was nearly eleven and it had damaged her leg, but she went on to become an Olympic champion at the 1960 Games in Rome. She became the first American woman to win three gold medals in track and field during a single Summer Olympics and was considered to be the fastest woman in the world during those halcyon days of her fabulous career.

Sadly, she died only two years later, at the age of fifty-four, after battling brain and throat cancer.

| AN AMERICAN TOUR

Returning to New York, the place of my birth and a city of which I have many warm memories, is always emotional for me. But it was particularly emotional going back there so soon after my mother's death for the American World Cup in 1994.

I remember wondering, 'Imagine what she would have thought about me being back here doing the World Cup for television!' She was funny in her own way. She would tell me that on plane journeys back and forward between New York and Dublin the Aer Lingus steward would say to her, 'You look familiar. You wouldn't be related to Jimmy Magee, by any chance?' I always knew that this was a little fib and that in fact she was probably telling them that she was Jimmy Magee's mother. I would have been pleased if she did say that, as it showed how proud she was of me.

As I strolled through the streets of New York in 1994 I also thought to myself, 'Imagine if I had I stayed in New York. What would have happened if my mother and father never went back to Ireland? Would I be covering this World Cup at all? Possibly not. Or would I be doing it for one of the big American television networks and having a limo with a driver of my own, and my own PA? Or would I be driving the bloody car for someone else?'

There was no knowing what I would have been doing. I said to myself, 'Amn't I a lucky man to be doing what I wanted to do, and getting paid for it.'

And then my mind wandered back to all those years ago when my children were still young and I was offered a job on a music station in Akron, Ohio, the fifth-largest city in the United States. The offer had come when I had my own show called 'The Golden Hour with the Millionaires' (the show that later became 'The Golden Hour' with Larry Gogan). It dealt solely with records that sold a million and was on for an hour every night. This executive from the American station was driving through Ireland and heard the show and liked it so much that he made contact with me, saying he had heard I was big into sports, and asking me if I would be interested in going to work for him.

I was torn, but turned it down. I nearly took it, but stupidly I said to myself that I wanted my children to grow up in Ireland. It was as if I thought somebody would chew them up and spit them out in America. I have no regrets about it, but if I knew then what I know now I would have accepted the job. I don't lose sleep over it, but it was one of those 'what if?' moments that crossed my mind during the 1994 World Cup.

The tournament didn't start promisingly for me. I had one of the scariest experiences in my life. I was in my hotel room, and when I went into the bathroom my nightmare experience began. I always close the door when I visit the bathroom; even if I'm in a room on my own I insist on closing the door. But it was to my own detriment on this occasion.

I shut the door and did whatever I had to do and cleaned up. In a few minutes' time I was to meet a colleague, Andy McKiernan, down in the lobby to go off to a game together. I went to pull the bathroom door open but it wouldn't budge.

At first I didn't panic. I tried it again, and it wouldn't open. I verified that it was locked and tried opening it and then attempted to pull it again. It wouldn't open. 'Janey Mack!' I muttered.

This was at a time when most people didn't possess a mobile phone. I frantically looked around to see if there was a phone in the bathroom—as if! I had no way of enlightening anyone about my predicament. Panicking, I began knocking on the walls in the hope that there would be a hotel employee around somewhere.

Minutes passed, and there wasn't a sign of anybody. I began wondering how long the air would last. All these things were now running through my head. 'How much air have I left? Will I ever be found?' The guy waiting downstairs for me would know that I'm always on time, I reassured myself, and he'd be wondering why I wasn't there and he would come looking for me. After all, in emergencies it's always best if you try to concentrate on positive thoughts.

If I could only get the door slightly ajar I knew I could get it open. 'How am I going to do that?' I mused.

I noticed that there was a little sliver of light creeping into the bathroom through a crack—maybe a quarter of an inch. 'I'll get something in there,' I thought. So I took a facecloth, and it took me ages to get it wedged in underneath. After I had pushed it in there I thought, 'If I could get another one and put it in it will eventually force the door.' So I kept doing it, and eventually, after a long struggle, the door popped open. The sweat was pouring out of me after this epic battle with the bathroom door.

When I eventually got down the stairs Andy was laughing when he saw the sweat pouring from me. I said to him, 'You're some colleague!' And I told him what had happened, and he laughed more. He then said that he was wondering where I was because I was always on time. 'I thought you must have had a bird up in the room!'

'It's a good job I hadn't, because I only had enough air for one!'

———

The tournament could only go one way for me after this—and that was up. The US '94 World Cup will not go down in the annals of history as being one of the best for presenting quality soccer, but it was one of the most enjoyable for me on a personal and a professional level.

I travelled extensively across the United States to cover games in different groups. The group A opening game, between the United States and Switzerland, was the first World Cup match to take place indoors, played under the roof at the Pontiac Silverdome.

The Colombian defender Andrés Escobar scored an own-goal against the United States, and his side lost 2-1, which resulted in them being placed bottom of the group. It turned out to be the group of death for the footballer nicknamed the 'Gentleman of Football', for ten days after his return home he was shot dead outside a bar. He was shot twelve times at close range. It was thought that a drug cartel had had him murdered, in retaliation for the own-goal, which had cost them heavily at the bookies.

The '94 World Cup will also be sadly remembered for Maradona being unceremoniously booted out of the competition, never to play on the world stage again, after he tested positive for a 'cocktail of drugs', including ephedrine, a weight-loss drug. I had a camera crew with me the day he was suspended, and I asked the man who was sending him home, 'What did he take, or was it a combination of stuff?' And that's when the phrase came out, that it was a 'cocktail of drugs'. I was the person who got the quotation that all the papers went with.

That happened in Dallas, and the next day I had to get an early-morning flight to Washington. After my plane touched down I booked in to the hotel and then went straight out to a pharmacy. I asked for the person in charge, because I felt I had to find out about this drug.

The head man came out, and I asked, 'Can you tell me what these things are?'

He tried his best to explain that they would help to reduce weight, and about sleep patterns, etc.

'Would I lose weight if I took them?'

He looked at me and laughed. 'Well, you would want to take the whole shop to do it.'

Then I asked him if it would affect performance.

'No, I can't see it. Well, it would affect performance all right if you lost weight, but you couldn't lose weight in a day and then perform better.'

I explained that I was a journalist covering the World Cup and that a man called Maradona (he had never heard of him, making him the best chemist I could have gone to) had been expelled.

I wrote a piece about it and how Maradona could have been just a scapegoat. Now, I'm not saying he didn't take the stuff, and I'm not suggesting it wasn't illegal, but I felt that if he was at it then others were probably at it also. But they needed to get a big scalp, and Maradona was the biggest scalp you could get, just as Ben Johnson was in the 1988 Olympics. I do believe Johnson took stuff, but then when he was stripped of his gold medal and everybody behind him was moved up one slot, if you look at their subsequent cvs those athletes were not lily-white at all.

Personally I was disappointed not to have Maradona there on the world stage. At the very least he would have brought some excitement and much-needed skill to the tournament.

After doing the commentary on the opening game in Dallas I went straight onto a flight the next day for San Francisco, and the day after that to Washington for yet another game. It was unbelievable stuff, but I wasn't the only one doing that type of extensive travelling.

I was delighted to be on the roster for the commentary on the Irish game against the Netherlands in Florida, where my younger sister, Pat, lived. I had been disappointed not to get the Italian match, as it would have been fantastic to cover Ireland playing a game in the city of my birth. Well, the game was technically in New Jersey, a different state but only a stone's throw from Manhattan. We had a great match in the Giants' Stadium, and I don't think anybody will ever forget Ray Houghton's beautiful chip over the head of the Italian goalkeeper, Pagliuca, that ended up in the net. He will also be fondly remembered for his header against England in Euro '88. But it was fantastic to get one over on the Italians after they beat us in the quarter-final of the previous World Cup by the same score of 1-0.

It was a very tight group, with all four teams—Mexico, Italy, Norway and Ireland—ending up on four points. It was John Aldridge's goal against Mexico that got us ahead of Italy and Norway and out of the group.

Some of our performances were absolutely terrible. But again the argument put forward was 'The end justifies the means.' Alas, no, for me it does not. If I was the trainer, yes, the end would justify the means; but if I'm a paying spectator it does not. I know that's something of a contradiction, but it's the truth. Who in their right mind wants to be bored to death by an unexciting game?

Anyway, there was no justifying our performance against the Dutch. Yes, there is the excuse of the hot weather, but the Dutch had to deal with it too. FIFA should have demanded that games like this be played in the evening, but they were obviously more concerned about scheduling the games to please the television stations. There was no way we were going to be able to play our pressing game against the Dutch as we had against the Italians in New Jersey. It says a lot about the quality of our players back then that they were officially the only team to beat the Italians in that tournament: the Brazilians won the final itself only by beating the Italians on penalties.

As soon as the match against the Netherlands kicked off, all I was thinking was, 'Here we go again!' Paul McGrath got what looked like a goal but was penalised because his boot made contact with Frank Rijkaard's head. Paul was special too: he was a great player in that championship. He will never be forgotten in Ireland. I will always remember being at Lansdowne Road and hearing the fans shout, 'Ooh, ahh, Paul McGrath!'

I have always got on well with Paul, and it would pain me to watch him destroy himself with his heavy drinking. I've met him in his worst states. I meet him quite regularly and I was always giving out to him about the drink. I would say to him, 'Do you know these people who buy you drinks, Paul? They might as well be sticking knives into your liver. You might think they're your friends, but they're not.' And he would tell me that he knows. I would urge him that every time they come looking for him to go off for a drink he should make up some excuse. 'Pretend you're sick or something, but don't accept a drink.'

And again he would tell me, 'I know, Jimmy.' Then he would tell me that he's heading off to meet a few friends but promises not to drink, and I would see him a few hours later and he would be trying to skip away from me so I wouldn't catch the smell of booze on his breath. I would say, 'You were at it again!' and he would barely reply that, yes, he had hit the bottle again. I couldn't get through to him.

Amazingly, the boozing didn't seem to impair his performances on the pitch. I went to a match in Stamford Bridge to do the commentary on Chelsea playing Aston Villa, and there was big talk for days before the match that McGrath wasn't playing because he had been on the tiles. I went down to the dressing-room before the match to check the teams. Ron Atkinson was the manager of Villa at the time. I asked him, 'Is the big man playing today?'

'Well, he's in there at the moment trying to put on his shirt, and if he gets it on he's playing.'

He was actually jarred in the dressing-room, but Atkinson thought so much of him that he was willing to let him go out and play. I didn't talk to him in the dressing-room; I decided if he was like that it was better to stay away.

He actually got the Man of the Match for that game. According to Paul's own book, he doesn't remember playing that match. He remembers being picked and doing his best.

The Irish players and the Irish people loved him. I think we love rogues.

Paul is a very quiet man. He's a lovely singer too. He sings in tune and in time, and he sings lovely, gentle romantic songs. Thankfully, at the time of writing he has been dry for almost a year.

Chapter 13 ～

BOXERS, IN AND OUT
OF THE RING

I've been fortunate not to meet too many rude sportspeople. I can count on the fingers of one hand the number of negative experiences I've had, which is probably rare enough in the sports world.

My biggest run-in occurred in Manchester in 1996 with Nigel Benn, who was the world boxing champion at the time. He had just lost to Thulani Malinga by a twelve-round decision, which lost him the WBC world title, but he was given a chance at the WBO's world title. Steve Collins was to fight this tough and rough Londoner for the world title. The fight was being sponsored by Beamish, who had brought the Irish media over to Manchester for the press conference.

Benn was more than half an hour late, which made the British press pack furious. It was a tense press conference: the journalists were narky with Benn, and he responded in a similar fashion, with curt and hostile answers.

When the press conference ended I approached Benn. 'Nigel, I'm Jimmy Magee from RTE television in Ireland. Will you do an interview with me, please?'

'No,' he snapped.

'It would be just a short piece. Just a few quick questions.'

'No!' he shouted.

I couldn't believe how rude he was being to me, without any provocation. Without saying another word I turned around and walked away. As I did I thought to myself, 'He has some bloody neck. We came specially over here for him and he won't even bloody talk to us. It's the height of ignorance.'

Standing outside the hotel, I saw Benn come out the door, and I thought, 'Now that the whole thing is over and he's clear of all his commitments I'll approach him again.'

I walked over to him and asked, 'Would you be able to do the interview for RTE now?'

'Didn't I already tell you no? So fuck off,' he said angrily.

'Who do you think you're talking to?' I didn't care that he was the middleweight world boxing champion: I wouldn't let anyone talk to me with such disrespect. Before he had a chance even to reply I told him, 'If I was twenty years younger I'd put you on your arse here and now.'

'You and your whole family, you mean,' he said, smirking.

'No—just me.'

Our raised voices had by now attracted a crowd around us. Steve Collins later told me that he thought he was going to have to 'step in there' to help me and fight Benn out in the car park!

After the confrontation I thought I really had some cheek talking to the world boxing champion like that. But the English media thought it was hilarious and congratulated me for putting Benn in his place. John Rawling of the BBC told me: 'All of us would love to have said that for years, but nobody had the courage to say it to him.'

I went off to sit on a little wall outside the hotel to calm myself down. I had my head down. I became aware of footsteps approaching me but didn't look up until I was addressed by the chairman of Beamish. 'Jimmy, I have someone for you to meet.'

I looked up, and he was standing with Nigel Benn.

'I'm ready to do that interview now,' Benn said.

'Ah, it's too late. The camera's gone,' I sighed.

'I'll go and get it,' Benn offered.

'Fine,' I said, nonchalantly. My enthusiasm for interviewing Benn had now completely and utterly vanished. But I smiled as I watched him dash off to find my camera crew. He eventually arrived back with them and we prepared to do the interview.

I thought about the time he was in the ring and he got down on bended knee to propose to his girl-friend. I was feeling very courageous now, and I said, 'I saw you doing something in the ring with your lady, and I want you to do it now for me and apologise.'

He got down on one knee—I'm not joking—and he apologised, looking into the camera. 'I'm sorry, Jimmy,' he said. But RTE never used it! It would have been a fantastic piece for the news.

After the apology I didn't carry on the interview. I told him, 'I've nothing more to say to you.' I was still vexed, and my heart wasn't in it. He had shown his true colours earlier. But we shook hands.

'And I don't think you'll beat Stephen Collins.'

Benn laughed and insisted he was going to knock out Collins.

On the night of the fight I was at the ringside and I watched Benn coming down the walkway, waiting for his call to get into the ring. He was looking around, and when he noticed me he smiled and said, 'Ah, you're here.'

So he hadn't forgotten me in a hurry. I was delighted when Collins knocked him down in the fourth round. An immediate rematch was called. Benn gave the excuse that he had been hampered by an ankle injury; but Collins won the rematch the following November in the sixth round.

My scuffle with Benn seems to have become part of sporting folklore in England, because it's an incident that is always brought up by my media colleagues any time I'm over there covering an event. They seem to have got a kick out of how this older Irish broadcaster stood toe to toe with Benn. I'm glad they got a kick out of the story; and I'm glad I didn't get a punch for my troubles, which would probably have ended with Collins taking on Benn in the car park to defend my honour!

———

It amazes me how boxers, who are some of the toughest men, can also be the most courteous and friendly—apart from Nigel Benn, I hasten to add. I've been lucky enough to meet all the great boxers of the twentieth century. I did radio reports on the famous Muhammad Ali fight against Al Lewis in Croke Park back in July 1972. I know everybody remembers it fondly as this big fight. Yes, it was a big day, but it wasn't as full with punters as you'd probably imagine, or as impressive as I thought it would be. I suppose it's hard enough to fill Croke Park for an all-Ireland final, let alone Muhammad Ali and an unknown opponent. But Ali was great on that day.

I first met Ali in Dublin during that fight, and I met him a few times afterwards. I got to see up close how much his Parkinson's disease had destroyed him when I did a Q&A show with him in Dublin and he was hardly able to talk. It was only a short piece, and I answered most of the questions for him, because he was really only able to smile and nod. It was one of the saddest moments I ever experienced.

My fondest memory of Ali involved the 1996 Olympics in

Atlanta. For several years I have been doing the commentary on the opening ceremony of the Olympic Games, which are fantastic moments to be involved in. I love watching the parade of the teams, and you don't know who is going to ignite the flame. If you wanted to find out beforehand you could, but I never wanted to: I wanted to find out at exactly the same time as the viewers and listeners, so I could respond in exactly the same way they do. When I saw Ali perform the opening ceremony in 1996 I thought, 'Oh, my God!' It was really emotional to see him back on the Olympic stage after he had thrown his Olympic medal into the river when he was refused service in a whites-only restaurant in his home city, Louisville. Here he was back in his native South opening the Olympic Games in Atlanta, the biggest event ever to happen in the Southern states. What must it have felt like for him?

Ali was the greatest boxer ever, but he was only slightly better than Joe Frazier. At the time they met in 1971 in Madison Square Garden they were both unbeaten. It was a unique situation to have two heavyweight world champions meet when they were both unbeaten.

So, you're probably wondering, how could they both be champions? Simple. Ali was the champion when he refused to serve in the US army. His licence was then removed and he became *persona non grata*. Eventually he was reinstated, not having lost in the ring. In the meantime Frazier became the world champion.

Frazier won the first and Ali won the next two, but there was almost nothing between them—but Ali was past his peak at this stage, it must be stressed.

Frazier was a nice man. I met him in Dublin when he came over with his rock-and-roll band, aptly named Joe Frazier and the Knockouts. He was the singer—a good one too. I have to doff my hat to him for deciding he was going to be a rock singer after retiring from boxing. He was playing in the National Stadium, which was also appropriate.

He was a pleasant man that day when we met backstage before his concert, but it was clear that he never really forgave Ali for the stuff he said about him. Ali had thrown some awful wounding remarks at him before the fights. It wasn't just the insults but the way he said them. The biggest insult to a black American is to call him an Uncle Tom; and Ali called Frazier an Uncle Tom. The emotional wounds from the insult were still raw after all those years, so much so that Frazier was reluctant even to talk to me about Ali. I understand that right up to his death he never forgave him.

––––

I met the boxing promoter Don King one evening at Kennedy Airport in New York up in the Aer Lingus lounge while waiting for a flight to Ireland. It was comical looking at him standing there talking non-stop on five or six different mobile phones. 'Get him! Get his ass!' he was shouting into the phone, and all that sort of nonsense. He was quite noisy. Anyway, we had a brief conversation about who was the best fighter ever, and the name that jumped out was Muhammad Ali, followed closely by Joe Frazier.

Of course his own client, Mike Tyson, was a great fighter too. Tyson did a show with us in the Burlington Hotel in Dublin in 2004. He was a colourful character, despite the fact that he is rough and ready. I had heard stories about how he could be rude and cause trouble when being interviewed, but I wasn't going to be afraid to ask him a question. Besides, he was being paid to be there.

At the show that night there was a young fellow from Co. Mayo called Henry Coyle, who was the Irish welterweight champion, and he had asked me before the event if there was any chance of meeting Tyson. I told him, 'I've no idea what mood Tyson is in, but I'll do what I can.'

When I was out on stage with Tyson I said, 'Mike, before we begin the show proper there's a young man in the audience who has asked me to introduce him to you.'

He grunted and asked unenthusiastically, 'Who is this guy?'

'He's a boxer, Mike—a real boxer like you. He's not a pro, he's an amateur, thinking of going pro.'

'Can I see him from here?' Tyson asked, sounding more interested now.

I pointed out Henry to him. Tyson began addressing Henry, looking straight at him. 'When you're going pro make sure your manager is proficient. Don't lose all your money, like I did. Don't listen to this one, listen to that one.' And he gave him a whole lecture and then bent down from the stage to shake his hand.

He talked about how much money he had earned—I can't remember the exact figure, but let's say $200 million. He said he had got something like that astonishing figure in purses, and what had he left? Nothing. He told of getting a purse for one fight of $20 million, but by the time he paid his manager, PR, sparring partners and miscellaneous hangers-on he said he still owed them a tenner!

Henry tells me he will never forget the moment. Last year (2011) he was boxing in Castlebar for a version of the world title, and he told me that night that he still tells people he met Tyson, and they don't believe him. 'But you're a witness that I met him, Jimmy, and he was so nice to me. He gave me great advice.' Which, in fairness to Tyson, he certainly did. And now Henry's meeting with Tyson is on the record in my book for any disbelievers.

———

I also had the opportunity to meet the great Sugar Ray Leonard when I was invited to present a Q&A evening with the legend at the Burlington Hotel. He was a very bright fellow in every sense. There was so much to talk to him about: he had met and fought all the greats.

There were five guys around at the time who were champions, and each one could be called an all-time champion: Sugar Ray, Thomas Hearns, Marvellous Marvin Hagler, Roberto Durán, and Wilfred Benítez; and each of them fought each of the others. Leonard had fought and beaten them all. At that time he was encouraging a young Irishman by letting him use his gyms in America. That young Irishman did him proud and went on to become a world champion. His name is Bernard Dunne.

At the 2009 world boxing championship in Milan I was doing commentary and interviews when I went from the ringside back to the press room, and standing in front of me was the former undisputed world middleweight champion, Marvellous Marvin Hagler, who spends most of his time now in Italy. In 2002 the magazine *Ringside* placed him among the top twenty boxing greats of the past eighty years, which is an amazing achievement when one even begins to think about the litany of fantastic boxers to be squeezed into the pantheon of all-time greats.

'Jimmy, how are you?' the American boxing giant said to me.

He was standing beside a woman whom he introduced as his Italian wife, Kay.

I was surprised that this legendary boxer remembered me.

'I guess I should call you Marvellous!' I joked.

'As you wish.'

'I'm surprised that you know who I am.'

'How could I ever forget the Irishman Jimmy Magee! I met you at many of my big fights, and you were always very kind, Jimmy.'

I thanked him. I was even more taken aback when he insisted on getting his photograph taken with me for his private collection.

It amazes me how some of the toughest men can also be the most courteous and friendly—apart from Nigel Benn, I hasten to add!

Chapter 14

DREAMS FULFILLED AND UNFULFILLED

A few days after Steve Collins won the first fight between himself and Nigel Benn I was packing my bags again and heading to Atlanta for the 1996 Olympics, which would turn out to be the most successful—and the most controversial—in the history of Irish athletics.

What's my take on the Michelle Smith controversy? I believe she didn't take any illegal substances, but I find people laugh at me when I say that. All I will say is that she was caught after she was out of competition and they found the sample to have been tampered with. At the Olympic Games she did all the drug tests and they were all negative.

I know everybody says her remarkable achievements had to be a result of performance-enhancing drugs, but I think this point I'll make will persuade you to have a rethink about it all.

I had a book of results at home, and I took it out one day and I took one of the events in which she won a gold medal and I asked one of my children: 'Have a look there at all those winners and tell me what you can see.' She said that all she could see was that those who had won the event before Michelle had all won it in a faster time than she had.

I asked my daughter if she didn't think then that they had

been taking something. She replied, 'No, but everyone believes it in Michelle's case, because she had improved so much.'

Yes, she had improved under the guidance of her husband and coach, Erik de Bruin, but the fact remains that she won in a time that wouldn't have got her first over the finishing line in previous Olympics.

I knew Michelle, and she is very annoyed at how she was treated, but can you blame her? She is still the champion; she has never been deprived of her medals.

That night was one of Ireland's greatest sporting moments. As Michelle was coming out of the athletes' mixed zone, as they call it, I said to her, 'You're going to be the most famous Irish sportswoman of all time.'

When she was at the press conference she was very mannerly, while the Americans were very unmannerly in the way they asked the questions. In the middle of it all up pipes Seán Bán Breathnach and asks Michelle a question in Irish. She answered in Irish, and that caught the Americans by the knees; they were now wondering what they were saying to each other. I thought that was a beautiful moment.

It was all sour grapes on the part of the spoiled American brats, who felt it was their God-given right to win on home soil. We must also remember that President Bill Clinton apologised for the American swimmers' insulting innuendos at the time.

I keep repeating myself, but she took all the appropriate tests at the Olympics, and not one of the results showed any trace of anything illegal.

Michelle later studied for the bar and finished in the top handful in her exams and is now a practising barrister. Your honour, I rest my case.

In 1995 a contact from the Ulster Council of the GAA approached me and asked me, 'Would you consider doing Gaelic games?'

'I'd love to, but I probably won't get them in RTE now,' I replied. In fairness I should add that RTE had a man in place already for finals. I said it had always been an unfulfilled dream to do the commentary on an all-Ireland final in Croke Park—something I had dreamt about ever since I was a young boy listening to the wireless.

A short while later I was doing 'Know Your Sport' in Monaghan when a UTV executive came over and said to me, 'We know how eager you are to do Gaelic games, and we'd love you to do the Ulster championship for UTV.' It so happened that the contract for Gaelic games had only recently changed from BBC to UTV and they hadn't got anyone signed up yet as the main commentator. I was told they were going to propose me, and I said that that 'in principle' I would like to do it.

A short while later I got a phone call from someone in UTV asking me, 'Jimmy, do you ever be up in Belfast?'

'Funny enough, I'm in Belfast next week.'

I gave them a call when I got there, and we went for lunch and we thrashed out a deal, and then a couple of days later I signed a contract. One of the things I always wanted to do was an all-Ireland final, and UTV were offering a deal that would see me do six all-Ireland finals in three years.

The powers that be in RTE were not deliriously happy with the news that I had signed a contract with UTV, but, thankfully, they never severed my connection either. I was told before I signed that it would 'rule me out of various things.' You make your bed and lie in it, but I always felt part of RTE. I wouldn't let anyone run them down.

But I had being doing 'Know Your Sport' for eleven years, and I was taken off that because of my deal with UTV. The head of sport at the time in RTE said to me, 'We'll have to take you off "Know Your Sport".'

'Why?'

'It's the opposition,' he replied.

I couldn't fully agree with it, but I had to go along with it. I was told I was 'their man' and they didn't want me appearing on a rival station. 'There's only a very small pot of advertisements and all that and we're competing in the same field with UTV.'

In fairness to him, he said, 'I'll tell you what I'll do. You can stay on and do all the questions and background stuff for the same money.' Of course I said yes. But I lost appearances, which in itself is money really.

I have no big grief about that. So when the three-year contract with UTV was over, RTE took me back without any residuals at all. Perhaps naïvely, I hadn't thought that there would be a problem, because I had previously done some Gaelic matches for Channel 4, which would send my feeds to Sky, and RTE didn't mind that—but that was obviously because Channel 4 is a British station and, unlike UTV, is not a direct competition for local advertising in Ireland.

I also did some boxing and soccer for the BBC in the 1960s. Again, in fairness to RTE, I must say that they didn't mind me doing it, as it was only the occasional bit of work.

———

I think my favourite freelance gig of all time was working with

Europa in the Netherlands, which was the forefather of the present Eurosport, done by a combination of national television stations. They asked me to do a piece on sport, and I must have done it well, because it was extended and extended and I ended up going regularly over to Hilversum for about four years to work for them. I actually got the contract through a fellow in RTE, as they used a lot of RTE people. They needed someone who could do it in English and I was recommended.

I would go out on a Tuesday, be met at Amsterdam airport by my own driver, who would drive me to Hilversum. If it was around lunchtime we would stop somewhere *en route* and chat over a bite to eat. We would then arrive at the studio and my bags would be sent over to the nice little hotel I always stayed in.

One particular Tuesday when I arrived there I went and did some editing for a football programme that was going out that night and then had to go to London to do a boxing match. Then I flew back to Amsterdam the morning after the fight and that evening went to Madrid to do a football match, and was then back the next morning to do some editing on the other European matches, and then I flew back to Dublin to work all weekend. That was a great buzz, even though it was very tiring.

Sadly, Europa went out of business—though for a very good reason, in my humble opinion, because as a station they tried to be all things to all. A typical evening's schedule at Europa was something like this: 7 p.m., a programme about religion; 8 p.m., a programme about the great art galleries of the world; 9 p.m., a music programme; 10 p.m., sport; and so on. So you just got the viewers for the specialist programmes and then they would click off. A television station needs loyal viewers to help make it an attractive proposition to potential advertisers.

In the early 2000s I had intended to start my own radio

station—a real sports station, doing nothing but what it says on the tin. Why? I wanted to have a lot of stuff that would have an interest for young people, because I feel that young people get interested in sports only by having positive vibes, positive commentary on sports, instead of the negativity and propaganda that you get these days.

When I delved into the possibilities and the financial side of it all I realised sadly that it just wasn't possible. Potential investors all said the same thing: 'Jimmy, it's a brilliant idea, but we can't actually see it making money.' It was a dream, really— perhaps 'fantasy' is a more apt description.

However, if I had my own broadcasting outlet, the first man I would try to sign would be Darragh Maloney, the best all-round man in the business. As a studio presenter and play-by-play commentator, he should be on prime pay.

———

After the Summer Olympics my next port of call was the 2006 Winter Olympics in Turin. I love the Winter Olympics. I had been at them before, in Innsbruck in 1976.

I got into a taxi in Turin and I asked the driver, 'Do you support Torino or Juventus?' Juventus is the most popular Italian club in the world but in Turin itself not necessarily; it's a bit like comparing Manchester United and Manchester City. It's said that more Mancunians follow City than United.

'I . . . am . . . Juventus,' he said.

'Liam Brady?'

'Ah! Liam Brady! You . . . amico . . . with . . . Liam Brady?'

I told him I was indeed a friend of Liam Brady. He left me at the main railway station, and he refused to take any fare, because I was an 'amico' of the great Liam Brady. It just shows you the reverence in which he was held in Italy.

I later recounted this to Liam and he grinned, 'Did you get the number of the taxi, because I'll be back there shortly!'

The first time I met Liam Brady was when I was over in Leeds visiting John Giles, who is a great friend of mine. I went to Elland Road one day to see Leeds playing Arsenal. Giles was the key player in centrefield for Leeds, but playing for Arsenal in the same position was a long-haired young fellow called Liam Brady, who stood out as a top-class player. I knew immediately that he was on his way to becoming one of our most important players—as apparently did John Giles, who was the Irish manager at the time.

I waited until the teams showered and changed, because I was travelling with Giles. We got into his car in the car park while the Arsenal players were getting on their bus. 'Hold on a second,' John said to me, and he jumped out of the car and ran over to the Arsenal bus.

'Liam, can I speak to you for a minute?' I heard him say. They had a brief conversation, but I didn't know what they were chatting about.

John returned to the car and I asked him, 'What do you think of Liam?' I really wanted to ask, 'Will Liam make the next Irish team?' But I would never invade his privacy—that's another very important thing. I would never ask him anything about his team or his team members; if he wanted to tell me stuff, that was fine, but I wouldn't expect him to tell me.

'I spent enough time being close to him on the pitch to know what he was like as a player. You'll find out soon enough that he'll be on the next Ireland squad.'

And sure enough, in the next Irish match Brady was playing centrefield with Giles. So I can say I was there the night Brady was auditioned, right beside the man who was picking the Irish team at the time!

I'm friendly with lots of footballers and hurlers, but I was really close in those day to John Giles and would often stay at his house in Leeds when I went over there to cover matches. I have vivid memories of his wife, Kay, always making big heaps of delicious chips for us—something that would be frowned on today by the dieticians at the big clubs, but it never adversely affected Giles's performances.

He was without doubt one of the greatest players to don an Irish international jersey. I had first heard about Giles when he was a schoolboy from his future wife's brother, Paul Dolan, who worked with me in 'Junior Sports Magazine'. Dolan, who was an Irish Olympian 400 and 200-metre sprinter, came into the studio and told me, 'You have to see this young guy playing. He's a genius.'

I went to see him play a couple of times. He was a little fellow—they were all little fellows, but he was little little. Yet I knew immediately that I was watching a genius. I then got to know Giles when he made it as a professional footballer over in England, first with Manchester United, and then we became more friendly when he went to Leeds United. He was brilliant at football, a brilliant man with a brilliant mind. Giles would respect you if he thought you knew something about football, or whatever subject you were knowledgeable about. He is a very solid person and a good, dependable friend. We don't get to talk as much these days, but I do see him occasionally when he comes over at the weekend.

Apart from soccer, John Giles is one of the best golfers I know. During the World Cup in Germany in 1974 he was there as a guest of the Brazilian Football Federation, because of his fame as a European footballer. He looked me up when he arrived in Frankfurt, which was our base for the competition.

Our meeting in Germany all those years ago is still a stand-out moment, because of our golf games. We decided to team up as golf partners, Giles-Magee, and we would meet two other guys and go for a game whenever we could. We would meet different people each day and we would always win, because Giles was brilliant. He could beat them out of sight.

One day we played a championship course in Frankfurt, and when we came to a section of the course where there is an up hole and a down hole parallel to each other, Giles said to me, 'You might be tired walking up the hill. Why don't you sit there and I'll try and hold the two other boys, and when we come back down you can have a shot at the next hole.'

He gave me a wink and headed off. Time dragged, and there was no sign of them. 'Where the hell are they?' I wondered. About twenty minutes later he was back down again. He told me that he won one of the holes and halved the other one.

'It's your turn,' he said.

I hit the ball and knocked it up to about five feet from the hole, and knocked it in for a par. Giles thought this was great and that they wouldn't match it. So now we were three up, which was really good. They couldn't believe it and promised they would get us the next day.

The next day we played against the trainer of the Leeds team, Les Cocker, and the day after that they had the number 1 golfer in Denmark; but not one of them could beat us, because Giles was on fire.

One day Giles said, 'See the top of the trees there? See the way the leaves are blowing? This is a dog-leg hole. Put the ball into them as high as you can and don't worry about it.'

The others were up first and they drove their balls, and the wind brought them right into the wood. I did as Giles suggested and our two balls went the far side of the wood. It was just brilliant coaching from Giles—and that was just at golf!

I also got to see him up close operating as a football manager when he took over as player-manager at Shamrock Rovers when my son Paul played for them. Paul made this step up to the League of Ireland after four or five of the lads from his team, Cherry Orchard, were block-signed by Shamrock Rovers during Giles's first season. And I must add that Paul wouldn't have told Giles that he was Jimmy Magee's son.

Paul was a very good striker, and Leeds United and Birmingham both wanted to sign him when they saw him playing with Shamrock Rovers. He was in the League team that won the cup with all these Irish internationals: Dunphy, Giles, Eoin Hand, Mick Gannon and Pierce O'Leary (who later became an international). That was a great team, which should have done better.

I did the commentary four times when Paul was playing. There was a certain amount of pride there and hoping he would do well—not fall over a ball or miss an open goal, which thankfully never happened. If I wasn't working I would go and watch him play. Paul never got booked—not even a yellow card—which is amazing when you consider that he would have been kicked around, as all strikers are. His motto was, 'If you can't take it, you shouldn't be out there.'

I was taken aback one day when John Giles and Ray Treacy came to the house and said, 'We're going to do something tomorrow. We're going to leave Paul out of the team and we're going to ask him to play with the B team.'

'Sure you don't have to come and tell me that. It's your club; you play it the way you like.'

They explained that they were going to play him at centre-half. They had something in mind, and at half time they took him off the B side and told him he would be playing for the first team the next day at centre-half. They were short a centre-half, and they had wanted to test him. He played so well in centre-half that he got man of the match in the papers. The two Rovers centre-halfs at the time were Noel Synnott and Johnny Fullam, but one of them was injured and the following week he was still out, and Paul continued in defence.

After a couple of weeks he was back, but then the other defender went out injured and he was out for a couple of weeks. So Paul had a long run at centre-half. It was actually in this position that Birmingham fancied him. He thought about going, but I told him I didn't believe it was a wise move, because he was struggling with a hamstring injury. 'What if the injury doesn't fully clear up,' I pointed out to him, 'and you went over there and were then turfed out?'

I think he made the right choice, because the injury did worsen, and he might have become surplus to requirements. Besides, he was a home bird anyway.

He was only in his mid-twenties when the injury occurred. He couldn't wait for it to clear up, because he wanted to play. But our hunch came true and the injury did cut short his career playing League of Ireland. So he decided, of his own volition, to give it up and went on to play instead with the local team in Stillorgan, alongside his brother, Mark. He could still have kept playing at the national level—he was very quick with the ball and very fast and strong—but when he had the injury looked at it was discovered that it was gone right up the back of his leg. It was operated on, but it never really cleared up properly.

Mark was a fantastic all-rounder and was amazingly fast. Both of them came on trips to America with the All-Stars.

———

It was through my friendship with John Giles that I also got to know Jack Charlton. It was a contact that would be very helpful in later years when he became the Irish manager. We first got to know each other during his Leeds days, and after the matches John would bring me along for post-match drinks with the other players.

Whenever I'm reminiscing with Giles about the times I went out with the Leeds players we always get around to mentioning what we call the 'Greek tragedy' episode. After a European Cup match in Saloníka the Leeds teams were invited to a cabaret. It was one of the funniest cabarets ever, because they had obviously gone out on the highways and byways and got three acts to come in and do their thing for these eejits coming in.

The first act came out and did a song, then introduced a woman who came out and did a song and went back in and then out again—just the three of them trying to do everything. Without a doubt it was the worst cabaret you could possibly see in the worst village hall in the world.

Through my friendship with Giles I got to know their legendary manager Don Revie very well. He was very kind to me. I would go to the ground, like an innocent boy, and he would always come over and ask how I was. And then he would get somebody to 'go and tell John that his friend Jimmy is here'. I might have only gone over to Elland Road a couple of times a year but they all knew me, and it was good for my morale that people at the top level of the game would accept me into their circle.

Like Giles, I was sad to see Revie leave the club. I know Giles got upset about the film *The Damned United,* based on the book by David Peace, and he successfully sued to have scurrilous passages in the book removed. He was depicted as the ringleader of the anti-Clough campaign. Now, I think it's fair to say that probably none of them liked Brian Clough, but I think the fact that he was Irish made him a juicy character for the book. Giles didn't really moan to me about him, because Clough was only there for forty-four days, so there wasn't really a lot of time to moan.

I met Clough once for dinner with the late Brian Moore on the eve of a cup final in London. Brian was a really nice man, while Clough was his usual abrasive self. He was quite nice to me, but I could sense why the Leeds players weren't enthusiastic about him, to put it mildly.

I met Norman Hunter some years later at a match in Elland Road and he was doing stuff for Leeds radio. I told him, 'I saw the old Leeds team on Sky Gold the other night and they were a marvellous team.'

'Yes, they were a great team. The thing about us was we had three or four natural left-footed players: myself, Terry Cooper and Eddie Gray. Then we had Paul Madeley and Billy Bremner, who were naturally right-footed. And then we had John, who could be anything he wanted to be.'

I thought that was the greatest tribute you could pay anyone. I told Giles about that and he seemed chuffed.

Chapter 15 ∾

| MUSIC MAN

I could probably be retired and sitting comfortably on my laurels if I had taken up a business opportunity with Garth Brooks!

Let me explain. I decided to go over to Nashville, because it's *the* place for country music. As a big country-music fan I wanted to visit the studios to see how the session men work, how they put songs together and how they record the singer with the band, which is not always the normal way of recording.

On one of my first days there I went to visit a country-music agent. She said she had a very good artist that she was trying to get going in Europe and wondered if maybe with my radio connections I could do something to help him break into Europe.

This agent was keen on the idea because of the precedent set by Nanci Griffith. She became big in Ireland first and then continental Europe and then got in the back door to become big in her native America.

The agent played me some of her client's tracks and I thought they were fantastic. 'What's the musician's name?' I enquired.

'Garth Brooks. He's going to be a major star, believe you me.'

At the time Brooks wasn't completely unknown in America,

but he hadn't completely knocked down the front porches.

'I've no doubt about that,' I said. 'Listen, I'd better tell you the truth here. These songs are fantastic. You have a genuine musical genius here; but I don't think I can be of much help in Europe. Yes, I have plenty of connections in Ireland and can do something there to open some doors for you. And I could probably do something in Britain. But there's no way I can do anything in Germany, because I just don't know anyone over there.'

I would be later kicking myself for not taking up the opportunity to be their European agent. Over the next eighteen months this little-known artist went on to sell $14 million worth of records, without me, and became one of the biggest names in music ever. Ten per cent on those figures would have set me up nicely.

I got to meet the man himself on my trip to pay homage to the musical greats of Nashville. The next time I was in visiting his manager Garth was passing through the office and he was called over and introduced to me.

'You're from Ireland? Wow! One day I want to visit your beautiful country.'

He seemed a genuinely happy man. The one thing that struck me was that he knew where he wanted to be going and he knew his present status and wasn't above his station.

I met him briefly once more in Dublin when he played here, which was a fantastic show. I have to say it was nice that he remembered me, and we reminisced about our conversation in Nashville and his dreams of making it big.

_____

In retrospect I think I should have told Brooks's people that I would take the gig and boasted about how I did have some experience in music promotion back in the 1960s when the 'twist' was all the rage. Leo Nealon, who ran the Irish Club in Parnell Square, Dublin and was an entrepreneurial figure, got me to go to London to try to track down a good Twist band and bring them on an Irish tour. I went over for him and I spent a lot of time in Soho, where the agents were based. I discovered an act called Peppi and the New York Twisters, and I arranged for them to come over to Ireland for a tour, which did really well.

Near the end of the Irish tour we arrived in Belfast one day to be met by a huge crowd of people on the street. Peppi couldn't understand it and thought they had a brilliant promoter who had all these people on the streets waiting for him. I hadn't the heart to tell him that the crowd was out for Louis Armstrong, who was staying in the Royal Hotel and also playing a concert that night!

I'm predominantly known now as a sports broadcaster, but in my early days I was known also for my music shows on Radio Éireann. The station used to stay open late for the weekly Hospitals Trust programme, which was a late-night show; otherwise the place closed at 11:30 p.m. I was the first to keep it open until midnight with a programme every Wednesday night sponsored by Spar called 'The Golden Hour with the Millionaires', about records that sold a million copies. Larry Gogan does the same show now, called 'The Golden Hour'.

It was my idea to start the Irish top ten chart show on RE, which began in 1962. I first had the idea when I was reading *New Musical Express*, which was the big music-industry paper. It always carried the British chart, and I thought, Where is the Irish chart? But there was no Irish chart, because Irish programmes played the music from Britain and sometimes the big American hits. Bit by bit I convinced RE that we should have an Irish charts show.

'How would I do it?' they asked me. I told them I had a way of doing it, by going to the manufacturers or distributors and asking them what their big sellers for the week were. I would then contact all the main music shops, county by county, and ask them the same. If it didn't coincide I knew there would be something wrong somewhere. I would take into account radio play and would balance the three together to create the charts. They agreed.

I was meticulous and conscientious about it; and Ireland's first top ten was broadcast in October 1962. The first number 1 was Elvis Presley's 'She's Not You'. The reaction from the station was good, and the reaction from the public was fantastic. There had never been anything like this before, and it's going ever since. It was a good first to have to one's credit.

———

On the subject of Elvis, I'm a huge fan of the King, to such an extent that I have paid homage to the man by visiting Graceland about five times. It's a fantastic place to go to, but I also found it quite eerie and it gave me goose bumps. I asked a couple of people if they felt something was present in Elvis's mansion, and they agreed that they too felt something—you just can't explain it in words, but it's as if you can feel the presence of Elvis still in the building.

Across the road from the mansion is the commercial side of things, where they have a studio with the backing tracks of all the Elvis hits, so you can record a number yourself. I did 'Are You Lonesome Tonight?' in the same key as Elvis.

The studio of Sun Records is also in Memphis, but for a building oozing history it doesn't look like much these days. The studio is just a room, but it's the fact of what happened there that is special. They have off-cuts of various things that happened, which are fascinating to listen to. The man who owned the studio, Sam Phillips, had only four artists signed to his label when he was starting off: Carl Perkins, who wrote and recorded 'Blue Suede Shoes' and sold a million; Roy Orbison; Jerry Lee Lewis; and Elvis Presley. Later on he signed Johnny Cash. That was his stable, which was just unreal. He had off-cuts of them all talking after recording sessions, some wonderful stuff, which I listened to on my visit.

The wall was covered with pictures of them, which I remember fondly, because it was almost exclusively that great era; but there was one other picture: an outsider's picture of U2. I got a great kick out of seeing them there on the wall of fame.

I went to Memphis to see all these things because if you are serious about music you have to know where these people came from. I was interested in all the places where music was performed, where it was written, who wrote it, who did this and who did that.

I also visited New Orleans to soak up its musical history. What a town! You go into Preservation Hall, a music venue in the French Quarter that was founded in 1961, and see all the old guys jamming, and you think to yourself, 'You couldn't get music like it anywhere.'

One of the first times I went there this young man, who had a young woman in tow, said to me, 'I know where you got 'em shoes.'

'I've no money; it's back in the hotel.'

'I don't want your money, man. I know where you got 'em shoes.'

'Really?'

'If I'm able to tell you where you got 'em shoes would you give me ten bucks, man?'

'I would.'

'I know your *goddam* shoes. Don't feel bad. You've just been had. You ain't the first and you won't be the last . . . You got 'em on your feet on Bourbon Street!'

I laughed, and I gave him the $10, as I thought he was worth it.

I met him the next day on the riverboat opposite St Louis Cathedral, and I said to him, 'I know where you got your *goddam* shoes . . .' and he laughed and said, 'Isn't it better than dealin' drugs, man?'

———

After launching Ireland's first music charts I got involved in the music business proper by becoming a minority shareholder in a record company. It came about because Mick Clerkin, who was the road manager for Larry Cunningham and the Mighty Avons, got a chance to start a record label, and he wanted me for the venture. It was a British label called King Records. Mick was smart, he could pick a hit; he mightn't be able to sing but he could pick a hit. He knew what the public wanted.

He had Larry on this label. He owned the company, and I had a little bit of knowhow that helped a little bit. I was only a small shareholder, but I didn't care about the lack of monetary gain, because I was learning all the time from the experience, as was Mick. We were all learning as we went along.

I enjoyed immensely being part of the label and being asked by Mick to pick out records that might be hits. We seldom missed: we knew what would go well, and then the nearly-all-right ones would go on the B side, so we had a strong product line.

Eventually King Records went out of business, but Mick was determined to stay in the music business and open a new record label. I told him, 'I've a great name for the record company: Release Records. It will be the most-mentioned name on the air, because with every new record being played the DJ will say, "This is the most recent release," or, "Newly released".'

The venture was a success, and we had enormous hits with the likes of Larry Cunningham and Dermot Hegarty. In fact so many people came onto the label that we launched another label, and then another one for the lighter stuff and the comedy stuff. Brendan Grace was signed up, as was Brendan Shine. We did tours of America among other things. The label even recorded some songs that I wrote myself.

I've written about six songs that have been published. Dermot O'Brien, who captained Louth to the all-Ireland football title in 1957 as well as being a renowned musician, was the joint writer of my songs. O'Brien played beautiful piano; accordion was his instrument of public knowledge but he could play trombone, and he could sing in many styles. Our first hit, about twenty years ago, was entitled 'Gypsy Boy'. He was the melody man and I was the lyricist.

I also wrote a song called 'Connemara Rose', which has now been covered by four or five different artists, such as the country singer Mick Flavin. Dermot O'Brien again wrote the music. This particular song came about like that because Dermot said to me one day, 'I want to write an Irish song. It has to sound old but it also has to be new. How long would it take you to write the lyrics, Jimmy?'

'I suppose a couple of days,' I replied, which he couldn't believe, as he thought it would take longer. In fact I had it done that night.

> Well, I met a girl in Connemara,
> Far west from Galway town.
> Her blue eyes glow with beauty
> And her red hair flowin' down.
> She lives among the mountains
> Where the wild, wild heather grows,
> And her name is Kate O'Hara.
> She's my Connemara rose.

We had it on tape in a couple of days, and it ended up being a big hit for Dermot when it was released on the record label I was involved with. He played it when he went on a tour of America. At a concert in San Francisco in which the audience was full of Irish immigrants he had many requests to sing 'Connemara Rose', which had just been released that summer. People came up to him at the end of the night saying to him, 'Thank you for singing that. I remember my mother used to sing that to me,' or 'My granny used to know all the words.' One night a fellow said to Dermot: 'Ah, God, it brought tears to my eyes when you played "Connemara Rose".' I remember my mother and grandmother singing it.'

Hopefully by the time this book comes out my latest song will be ready to be released. I'm planning to sing it myself. This new song is the story of Irish show business and the showband scene. I wanted to do a song that would be a tribute to all the showbands and would give the listeners a sense of their history.

It starts with a scene where we're in the back room having a few jars and fellows are talking and remembering different characters and singers and saying to me, 'Jimmy, you were around a long time, and surely you'd remember these people?'

It's not a heavy song but rather a light, sensible but true-to-life song, with a blend of pop and country.

I reluctantly recorded it myself. This came about after a conversation I had with Dave Pennefather, who was the European manager for Universal Music. We were talking about who would be best to get to sing the song, and Dave said, 'What about Larry Cunningham?' It was a good idea, because Cunningham was one of the leading players from the showband scene; but, as I explained to Dave, 'I can't have Larry, as he's actually referred to in the song. Fellows can't sing about themselves.'

'Why don't you sing it yourself?'

'I can't sing.'

'Sure can't you hold a tune?'

'I suppose if you can keep a pitch and keep time there's not much in it.'

'I'll produce it, and you try and sing it.'

The song is called 'These Old Eyes Have Seen It All'. The music is from an old country song.

I saw the Clipper Carlton playing on the stage
I saw Miami roll when rock was all the rage
And the first to play on Christmas Day was the Royal in the Ulster
    Hall
    These old eyes have seen it all.

Larry Cunningham in Cricklewood jammed the Galtymore
Joe Dolan in his suit of white sang more and more and more
Big Tom praised 'Gentle Mother' and Mick Dell played 'Every Ball'
    These old eyes have seen it all.

Chorus:
These old eyes have seen it all
Red Hurley, Freshmen, Eileen and Brian Coll
And the dazzling hands of D. O'Brien
Answered the all-Ireland call
These old eyes have seen it all.

I saw Butch Moore when he walked the streets in rain
Pat McGuigan singing Europe long before young Barry's fame
I heard Ray Lynam singing country when George Jones phoned him
a call
These old eyes have seen it all.

Brendan Shine washed down Con's Lobby
On windows Sonny Knowles
The swing clarinet of New Orleans was surely Paddy Cole's
The Indians wore the war paint, and that's no sitting bull
These old eyes have seen it all.

Chorus
Joe Mac had us laughing as he beat the Dixies' drum
And T. J. Byrne and Connie were the ones who did the sums
Brendan Bowyer did the Hucklebuck
And Art Supple mimed them all
These old eyes have seen it all.

When JR was shot in Dallas TR climbed to number 1
Jumping Johnny told the Las Vegas crowds about his Noreen Bán
Dennis Allen lauded Limerick
Daniel ditto Donegal
These old eyes have seen it all.

| A NEW LIFE

I'll always remember 1996, for two reasons: firstly, for Michelle Smith's victories, and secondly, because it was the year that I began to have some health issues, which led to me having a triple heart bypass that almost finished me off.

I'm lucky to be alive today after enduring my triple bypass operation in 1999, which resulted in me being in a 'touch and go' condition, lying unconscious in intensive care for more than a week.

It was probably my own fault for not heeding the earlier warning signals coming from my body. I had given up smoking and boozing in the early 1970s, but, being a typical man, I have always been reluctant to go to the doctor when I was suffering pain. I could have made life a whole lot easier, and safer, if I had immediately got a thorough check-up when I first noticed that my health was deteriorating, some three years before my life-saving operation.

I would never have dreamt that I would have heart problems. Like everyone else, I always thought that it's something that happens only to other people.

I began to notice that something wasn't right when I was attending the 1996 Olympic Games in Atlanta. It wasn't that I was in pain, but I wasn't feeling my usual upbeat self and instead was down in the dumps and lethargic. Rather than my usual brisk walking style I was ever so slowly strolling towards the stadium to watch the games, and I wondered to myself, 'How am I going to make it through today?'

Clearly it was obvious to some of my colleagues that something was wrong, because the *Irish Times* sports journalist Johnny Watterson, who is a former Irish international hockey player, caught up with me and remarked, 'You're taking it very easy today, Jimmy.'

I shrugged and lied. 'I'm taking the time to smell the roses.'

I knew I was in trouble as I watched Johnny, who wasn't walking particularly fast either, speed past me.

I knew I had a blood-pressure problem and thought it was connected with this, so I decided to seek out a doctor when I got to the stadium.

As I continued at my snail's pace towards the stadium I began to mentally kick myself for one of the silly things I had done earlier that week: dashing back to Ireland for twenty-four hours to do the commentary on a GAA match. During this period when I was in the United States for RTE I was also contracted to UTV to do the commentary on GAA matches. Of course it wasn't RTE's fault that I was working for UTV, and it wasn't UTV's fault that I was working for RTE. I had thought as I was heading out there, 'If I don't raise a rumpus about this everything will work out.'

I said to the producer on site in Atlanta on the Friday, 'Any chance of having a day off on Sunday?'

'If ever a man deserved a day off it's you. You never ask for a day off. Have you ever had a day off in your life?'

'Very few.'

'Of course you can have it. Is there any Irishman boxing or anything that we'd need you for?'

No, there wasn't.

I did a fight in the boxing hall in Atlanta on the Friday night and then sneaked off in a taxi to the airport and boarded a transatlantic flight. When I arrived in Dublin I immediately jumped into a car and drove to Clones, arriving just in time to do the commentary on the Ulster football final.

When I was finished in Clones the man in charge in Belfast came on the headphones and said, 'Thank you, Jimmy; that was terrific. You were in great form. Wonderful. Thank you very much.' I was surprised that I hadn't sounded tired after all that travelling.

On leaving the game in Clones I headed to Belfast, where I was doing some filming for Sky, a summary of the Olympic Games, and then I turned around and went back to Dublin, stayed in the airport hotel, and got a flight to Atlanta that arrived at 9:30 a.m. local time, and I was back in the stadium for 1:30 p.m. to cover the athletics.

The producer came on the headphones and said, 'That day off did you good. You were sharp and fresh today.'

I never told him about my epic journey. What they don't know doesn't bother them, I thought as I took off the headphones. If I had told either UTV or the producer in Atlanta the truth about all my travelling I think one or the other, or perhaps both, would have said, 'Ah, Jimmy, you weren't at your best today.' Instead I got the plaudits. It shows that you should never tell people what they don't need to know.

But a few days later I was really regretting all this travelling. I was sluggishly walking up towards the stadium. I was knackered, and I just hadn't got the energy to get up a slight incline and into the stadium.

Eventually I got inside. I've always thought that if you're ever going to get sick you should get sick at a sports event. I enquired about getting my blood pressure taken, and when I was told to walk up the stairs I shook my head and explained that I was too weak to make it that far. The official suggested that I should use the lift, and I replied, 'I might not be able to walk as far as the lift. I'm really, truly not feeling the best here.'

As I was in the mixed zone, where athletes coming off the track can seek medical attention, I decided to seek out a doctor.

At the Olympics everyone is colour-coded, so I looked for the 'red man', which was the medic. When I spotted the red colour code I went over to him, waved my accreditation badge at him and said, 'Doctor, do you mind if I have my blood pressure taken? I don't feel very good.'

He took one look at me and said, 'Come with me,' and ushered me inside the barrier and laid me down on a stretcher. As I had expected, he told me that my blood pressure was very high. He gave me some medication and then said to me, 'You'll have to lie down to see if it will go down.'

After about ten minutes my blood pressure had gone down, but he was still clearly worried about me and told me, 'You'll have to stay there.'

'I can't,' I said, shaking my head.

'You don't understand. We might have to hospitalise you.'

'I'm afraid not. I'm working. I'm doing a commentary.'

He laughed out loud when I told him I was scheduled to do the commentary on a game in less than twenty minutes. 'Not today you're not!'

'What do I have to do to sign myself out?'

He told me he would get the head doctor, who then came down and allowed me to leave, on condition that every fifteen minutes someone would come and take my blood pressure. I agreed, on the condition that it could be done discreetly: the last thing I needed was someone in a white coat with a stethoscope hanging from their neck barging into the broadcasting box and demanding in front of everybody to see me and take my blood pressure.

I brought a young doctor with me and showed him where we could meet in twenty minutes' time. Then I went into the commentary box and got to work. I would see the young doctor down below and he would catch my eye, and at a suitable moment during the commentary I would whisper, 'I'll be back,' and then head out to get my blood pressure taken.

The doctor would come closer and closer to where I was sitting each time he was trying to catch my attention. There were about four of these check-ups, and it was beginning to become obvious to my fellow-commentator Greg Allen that something was up. Eventually, when we went into a commercial break, I had to alleviate Allen's suspicions by telling a white lie. 'You know that thing they had out about how athletes respond under pressure?'

'Yeah?'

'Well, now they want to find out how commentators respond under pressure, so they asked me to be a guinea pig.'

Thankfully, the young doctor eventually agreed to stop taking my blood pressure, and I went on for the rest of the Olympics. When I got home I went to my local doctor and he immediately put me on blood-pressure medication, which didn't unduly concern me.

During the 1998 World Cup in France I was having occasional little lapses that I knew shouldn't have been there— like when walking up stairs I would get out of breath, which can happen to a lot of people. It's natural enough, and I kept telling myself this. Besides, when I would get to my position in the stand I would recover instantly, so I thought nothing of it. There are loads of ways you can cajole yourself into thinking everything is fine. I kept it a secret, because I didn't want anyone worrying about me, and there was no way I was missing out on doing the commentary on the World Cup. Besides, I was always on top of my game once the whistle blows. As a friend of mine says, 'Once that red light goes on you go into another gear.'

I then had another scare in 1998 while I was walking down Fifth Avenue in New York. I became so unwell that it was impossible to ignore the pain, and an ambulance was called to take me to Lenox Hill Hospital, which is near the top end of Central Park. Even though it was absolute bedlam in the casualty department I received fantastic attention from the medical staff, who never once gave the impression that they were under pressure or stress.

Again I was told that my blood pressure was sky-high and that I was lucky I had checked myself in for immediate treatment, because it would have been very dangerous if I had ignored the warning signs. Once my condition was stabilised I asked to be released, but the doctor refused. They agreed to phone my specialist back in Maynooth to compare medical notes. After that they reluctantly released me. In retrospect I know I was only delaying the inevitable.

It came to a head in February 1999 when the pain became so difficult to deal with that, of my own volition this time, I checked myself in to the Blackrock Clinic and was seen by a cardiologist, Dr Peter Quigley, and was given an angiogram. He said they would monitor me and I was to come back early the following week.

I flew over to London that weekend to cover a game at Chelsea. When I was walking up the steps into the stadium's broadcasting box I was so out of breath that a man stopped and asked if I needed any help. 'Yes, thank you,' I said. I gave him my bag and he helped me up the steps. When I got to the top of the steps with the help of this kind man the BBC engineer on duty looked at me and asked, 'Are you okay, Jimmy? You look very pale.'

'I'm fine,' I lied. 'I'm just a bit out of breath from those bloody steps. I'm not as fit as I used to be. Don't mention this to anybody, okay?'

He assured me he wouldn't. I sat down for three or four minutes to catch my breath and then I got stuck in to the match.

When I got home I had an appointment on the Monday at the Blackrock Clinic. 'How was your weekend?' Dr Quigley asked me. 'Had you any pain during the weekend?'

'No, I had no pain. All was fine, really.'

'I think that's a lie.'

'Were you not listening to me at the weekend? I'm grand.'

Not paying any attention to my amateur diagnosis, Dr Quigley said he was making an appointment for me with a specialist, Maurice Neligan, but before that he wanted to do an angioplasty.

It's a painful procedure where a narrowed or obstructed blood vessel is mechanically widened. After an angioplasty you have to rest for a few hours, because you might bleed. My son Mark was with me, and when the cardiologist came back in I knew by his face there was something up.

'When is your next game?'

'Saturday.'

'I don't think so.'

He explained that the results of my tests showed that I needed a heart bypass. I tried in vain to explain that I could continue on without such an operation if I simply continued to take my medication. 'I'm going to do the match anyway.'

I thought I would have to wait for a bed, and that would take

My late son Paul and his son David walking into the unknown. Ger O'Driscoll captured this very special picture of one man heading for the next world and a young man stepping into his future. (*Courtesy of Geraldine O'Driscoll*)

A photograph that I treasure: the last occasion on which Paul stood on his own feet. He insisted on standing between myself and Mark, although wheelchair-bound at the time. (*Courtesy of Beta Bajgartova*)

All five of my children: (*from left*) Patricia, Mark, Paul, June and Linda, and three of my eleven grandchildren, Sinéad, David and Sarah. (*Courtesy of Beta Bajgartova*)

Congratulating Andy Lee after victory over Alejandro Falliga, 2008. (© *David Maher/Sportsfile*)

Seán Crowley (secretary) and Dominic O'Rourke (president) make me a presentation on behalf of the Irish Amateur Boxing Association.

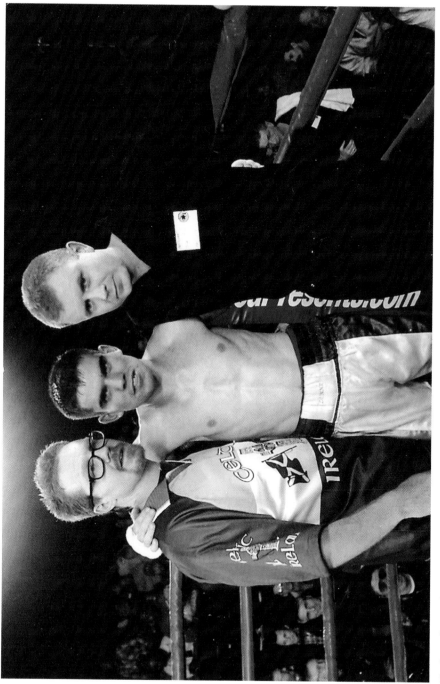

The legendary trainer Freddie Roche, Bernard Dunne and Dunne's manager and promoter, Brian Peters.

Launching the coverage of the 2008 Beijing Olympics, with Eamonn Coghlan, Katie Taylor, Bernard Dunne and Sonia O'Sullivan. (© Inpho/Lorraine O'Sullivan)

The Olympic silver medallist Kenny Egan and myself at the official opening of Neilstown Boxing Club, Dublin. (© *David Maher/Sportsfile*)

October 2010: When Ali met Jimmy, he won!

Meeting President Michael D. Higgins, with Seán Crowley, before the finals of the 2012 National Elite Boxing Championship. (© *David Maher/Sportsfile*)

weeks; so when I asked him when the operation would be I was taken aback when he bluntly told me, 'This Friday.'

'But I can't have it on Friday. I have the match the next day. I'm supposed to be going to Nottingham Forest v. Manchester United.'

I left the clinic insisting that I was going to England regardless. The next day the surgeon's secretary phoned me and said, 'Mr Neligan wants a word with you.' There was a pause, and Maurice came on the line. 'I heard you're going to the game in Nottingham.'

'Yeah. That's the plan. I'm determined to go.'

'Where's the commentary stand in the stadium? Is it at the top of the stands?'

When I told him they were on the roof of the stands he asked me, 'How will they get you down from there?'

'What do you mean? Sure they wouldn't have to get me down. They didn't have to get me down the last Saturday or the Saturday before. So why this Saturday?'

'Jimmy, I don't think you realise how serious this is. And you're still going to go? Fair play to you. I suppose I can't talk you out of it?'

'No, you can't.'

'Leave it with me,' he said.

He rang me back later that day. 'I've two phone numbers that you have to take down. Have you got a pen handy?'

I took out a piece of paper and a pen. 'Fire ahead.'

'This first phone number,' he began in his dry way, 'is for a friend of mine, a heart surgeon in Nottingham.'

I jotted down the number, starting to get where he was going with this conversation.

'I also want to give you the number for the Cardiology Unit in Nottingham General Hospital.' As he was reading it out to me he said, 'I think you'll need both of these.'

I'm only stubborn up to a point. I'm stubborn up to the point of no return, and then I de-stubbornise myself. If I make up my mind I stick to it; I don't think things on impulse. But this time I sighed and replied, 'Okay, Maurice. I've got the message now. I won't do the match.'

'Get yourself in here. We're going to have to do this operation as soon as possible.'

Petrified, I checked myself in to the hospital the following morning.

I was unbelievably nervous on the days leading up to the operation. I hate hearing the gory details of operations and other medical procedures, so the thought of somebody cutting me up—even if it was to save my life—had me frightened. I suppose it was because deep down I feared the unknown and hated having no control over what was about to happen to me. I didn't allow myself to think this was going to be the end, but I was nervous, because I didn't know what was in store. I didn't know what to think.

But I got some great moral support from my friends. Father Brian D'Arcy came into the hospital on the day before the operation to see me, and Bill O'Herlihy, who had also had a heart operation, came in to visit me. 'There's no use telling you that you'll be a new man tomorrow,' he said. 'This is not like cutting your toenails.' But he added that with my will power and general health I would get better, though it wouldn't happen overnight. I was glad he told me the truth, rather than feed me with rubbish.

Years later I did the same when Larry Gogan was having a heart operation. I went in to see him the day before it and he too was a wreck. I told him, 'I know what you want now: a big needle full of stuff to knock you out.'

He asked me, 'Will I be able to walk around like you in time?' And I reassured him that 'of course' he would. 'And sure I was playing football after mine.'

He tried to tell me I was different, but I wouldn't allow him to think like that and told him that within three months he would be better. He often says to me now that I was 'dead on'.

Ironically, I had the operation on the same day as the Nottingham v. Manchester United game. Before the operation I was told, 'We should warn you about this. You'll have a very strange kind of dream in the recovery room. This is a very serious operation, but in the recovery room you'll have some unusual dreams, to say the least.'

'What kind of dreams will I have?'

'It will be a mixture of fantasy and reality, but you won't notice the difference between them. Unlike normal nightmares, they won't be nightmarish but a mixture of reality and fantasy, but mixed seamlessly into each other.'

I certainly had post-operation dreams that seemed real and have been etched in my memory. The most unusual was one in which I was invited to an event in London and I arrived in a wheelchair with all the nuts and bolts sticking out of me. As I was wheeled into the room I recognised most people at it as being nearly all Irish celebrities from both the sports and the entrainment spheres. While I didn't know them all personally, I knew them from the screen, either television or films. Suddenly somebody screamed, 'Who let this smelly Irishman in here?' pointing at me.

And then two Manchester United players, Roy Keane and Denis Irwin—both of whom would have been playing in the match I was supposed to be doing on the day of the operation—along with the rugby legend Keith Wood, rushed to my defence. 'Don't you speak like that about Jimmy!' they said in unison.

Then Wood went up to the guy and they had a maul. Shortly afterwards the police were called and they fingered me as the ringleader of all this commotion.

I was trying to plead my innocence with the constable. 'How could I be the ringleader of anything? God! Just look at me!'

And then a voice appeared out of nowhere and said to me, 'Do you know where you are?'

'Indeed I do. I'm in Her Majesty's Theatre in the Strand and me and the boys are going to raze it to the ground!'

'No. The operation's been a success and you're alive.'

I realised that it was Maurice Neligan speaking to me. His was the first voice I heard in my new existence, my new life.

'Do you know where you are?'

I opened my eyes and struggled to smile.

I was later informed that my whole system broke down and my kidneys and other organs were failing. Usually after such an operation you'd spend about three days in intensive care, but when I woke up I discovered that I had been unconscious for about a week.

They were clearly nervous about me, which came through loud and clear when I woke up to discover that my sister Mary had flown over from America and was holding a vigil with other relatives at my bedside. I remember thinking, 'There must be something up here.' I'm open to correction on this, but I believe a priest may even have been summoned to give me the last rites.

They later told me that I was singing in my sleep in the intensive-care unit. A nurse asked Paul one day, 'How many songs does your father know?'

'Ah, sure you wouldn't know; he has a massive repertoire.

Sometimes he likes to sing "Summertime" and then he might do "Blueberry Hill". I've no idea how I was doing all this singing while I was knocked out.

Paul had some funny stories about me when I was unconscious in the hospital. He told me that somebody had wanted to visit me and I told them, 'I don't want any visitors. Unless it was the president they weren't allowed in.'

'The president of where?' Paul asked.

'The USA.'

I would then break into song again.

——

When I was in hospital DJ Carey came in to see me. I recounted a story to him about what Eddie Keher said about him. I did a quiz one night in the late 80s in Kilkenny with Eddie Keher, who appeared in six all-Irelands and was one of the most prolific scorers of all time. We were talking about the greatest players and he said, 'You love names, Jimmy. There's a young boy in Kilkenny and if he keeps at it and doesn't get ill and stays in love with the game he's going to be the greatest of them all. His name is DJ Carey. You should remember that name.'

DJ couldn't believe that Eddie Keher spoke so highly of him. He thought that was some tribute. 'I'm going to give you one now, Jimmy. There's another young fella coming along now who'll be better than any of us. So remember the name. The name is Henry Shefflin.'

Ten years ago I went into the Kilkenny dressing-room after they had just won the league and I went over and sat beside Shefflin and told him, 'I'm going to tell you a story about DJ Carey and Eddie Keher.' As I began to tell him I glanced over to the other corner and saw that DJ and Henry were actually in the room. After I'd finished Shefflin said, 'Did DJ Carey say that about me?'

'He certainly did.'

DJ was right too about Shefflin, who has just become the first player to win ten All-Stars, as well as eight all-Ireland medals, which is going to be an almost impossible feat for anybody to repeat. (In fact by the time this book comes out he could already be the only player to have a ninth all-Ireland medal.)

On another occasion I asked Ollie Campbell, one of the best out-halfs to play rugby for Ireland, 'When you were a young fella who did you want to be?' He told me he was always pretending to be Mike Gibson when he was playing as a young lad. The amazing thing was that his first cap for Ireland was against Australia.

It turned out that Gibson heard the story and either wrote to him or spoke to him to say how nice it was that he thought that much of him. I think it was great how they got to play as equals after Ollie had him as a boyhood idol.

I have a good story about when Ollie Campbell and Tony Ward were vying for the position of out-half for the Irish rugby team. They were probably the two best out-halfs in Europe at the time. Ward had a long stretch, and then Campbell had a stretch. Campbell, who owned a tie business, was driving in Co. Mayo one night coming home from work. There was a woman on the side of the road who had either missed her bus or was waiting on her bus, and he gave her a lift. They got talking about everything and anything and then sport. She said he looked like a young man who played sport, and he replied that he played rugby. She wasn't familiar with rugby and she told him the only thing she could say about rugby was 'I don't know why they don't play that chap Ward instead of your man Campbell.' What could Ollie say except 'I suppose you have a point'!

———

I cried bitterly after my heart operation. I had remained strong by not crying when my wife died, and would do so later after my son died—even though I was a broken man on the inside—but after the operation I broke down, because the sorrow came flooding back to me, and everything hit me at the one time.

When I finally got out of hospital I was determined to recover—and recover in time to be at the Olympics in Sydney in 2000. I walked around RTE with Noel Coughlan, who was the producer in charge for the Olympics, and told him, 'I'm going to the Games, and I don't want to be ruled out.'

'You won't be ruled out. I promise.'

RTE were very good to me then, but they were always good to me. They were trying to tell me to take more time off, but sure I wouldn't listen. In the end I went to Sydney. If you want to do anything you have to be determined.

I don't want to frighten anyone who is facing an operation such as mine, because these things can be cured, but it does take time. It took me three or four months to recover. I was in hospital for about a month. My family were very worried, which I can understand. I went back to work as soon as I could, which was about three months afterwards. I couldn't be lying around feeling sorry for myself.

I was supposed to do exercise, but I'm very poor at keep-fit regimes, though I did the occasional bits of walking. One of the places where I walked was UCD. I was walking there one day when away in the distance I saw a boy of about twelve kicking a football at the Gaelic posts and running back after it. Eventually the ball got stuck in a tree. I got up as far as him and he was throwing twigs and stones at the ball. I told him, 'Don't worry about it. I'll get the ball for you.'

I was still holding myself, because I had the layman's fear of the stitches bursting open. Without thinking, I jumped up and flicked it out of the branches. The young lad thanked me and I walked away. If I walked towards him at two miles per hour, that episode inspired me to walk away at six miles an hour. In one fell swoop I felt so much better. From then on I didn't allow it to become a 'lie down and feel sorry for yourself' issue.

When I was leaving the hospital I had asked Maurice Neligan what I thought was a perfectly natural question. 'How long will this last?'

'Listen,' he said, 'sit down there. When I had you opened up like the swing doors in a Western saloon you were at my mercy. And I got this piece of paper and I wrote on it, "This man will survive for ever".'

He paused as we both laughed and he continued: 'I stuck it into your chest, but I put the writing facing the back so that if they opened you up again they wouldn't be able to read it. In the unlikely event that you don't live for ever all the rest of us will be dead and gone, so they won't be able to blame us. So get out of here.'

As I was leaving, he told me he didn't want to see me again. That was thirteen years ago. Unfortunately he himself is now gone, and the fellow who did the anaesthetic is gone also. Maurice Neligan's funeral was a sad day for me, because I believe he gave me my life.

Chapter 17 ∾

| TIPS AND SLIPS

It's funny, but recently I was on a cruise and I got chatting to an Englishman about sport. He said, 'I bet you can't recall who won the FA cup in 1949.'

'I can. It was Wolverhampton Wanderers. And not only can I tell you that but I can give you the names of all the players,' and I proceeded to list the team and their positions.

This man, who didn't know me from Adam, said to me, 'This is amazing! You know what? They should call you the Memory Man.'

I didn't tell him that they already call me the Memory Man (whoever 'they' are)!

For the record, I don't get every question right. I have made an odd slip up and forgotten a name or date. Thankfully, however, even as old age creeps up on me I have retained this gift for sports trivia.

I haven't got a good memory at all: what I have is a memory for things I like, such as music, geography, travel and sports. Don't forget this was all pre-Google and all that, and if I didn't know something I'd have to look it up in a book.

People ask me if there is any secret or tricks to the Memory Man. Well, the answer is no. What you need to have is interest in the subject. If you have that you *want* to learn more about it. This applies to anything, like completing a Rubik's cube—

whatever you are interested in.

I was always interested in names and still interested in people's names to this day and trying to get them right. Pronunciation is very important: I often ask the person themselves how they pronounce their name. Memory Man is a thing that I think anyone can do if they apply themselves in any field: you have people who can tell you all the Beatles' hits, or how many number ones Elton John had.

I don't use any techniques, just an interest, so a whole heap of knowledge remains in my memory. I often test myself too. If I'm waiting for a meeting to start I have a habit of getting out a piece of paper and setting myself the task of writing down the names of those who played in a cup final—and not just their names but their positions too. Sometimes to pass the time I put together lists of teams. Nearly every piece of paper you would find in my pocket has a list on it of some description, from sports or music. On a long journey back from somewhere I would often wonder, 'Can I name all the British Open golf champions since 1946?' I'd be in the car on my own listing them off. I might miss one or two, but when I get home I look it up in one of my books.

I think this comes from this childhood thing of walking around and doing pretend sports programmes. It's a talent that must come from my fascination with commentary and the individual style and techniques of commentators.

What makes a good commentator? If somebody wants to get into broadcasting I would have some advice for them. During my long career I have thought a lot about what sports commentary is and the differences between commentators on radio and television. I think television commentary is identification and explanation, with occasional anecdotes thrown in.

I think statistics are overdone—I do them myself, but I hope I don't overdo them. They are useful but often they can be useless—saying something like 'That's Robbie Keane's fourth goal of the year.' I mean, what difference does it make what goal it is—the third, fourth or fifth; who cares? Yet all this stuff is trotted out, stuff like 'And that's his third corner this week.' It would be different if it was the first goal of the season, or his thirtieth goal of the season, or the hundredth goal of his career. In general I think commentary is being choked with statistics. I can give you as many stats as anyone off the top of my head, but I don't think I should be saddling everyone else with them.

Moving on to my thoughts on radio, I see commentary there simply as being a balanced mixture of description and geography. People should be told the geography of the pitch: where you are, the commentator, in relation to the pitch. You should set the scene. It's useful if people know the line-up of the pitch and where the grandstand is and so on. They may not know, and it's up to the commentator to say, 'There is one main grandstand, in which I am sitting, and an open side on the far side,' and off you go. For me the most annoying thing to hear from a commentator is 'The play is on the far side of the field.' What does that mean to the listener? Where is the far side of the field? All it means is that it is further from the commentator, but really the listener doesn't care how far it is from the commentator. What they should be saying is, 'It's five yards from the English goal,' or 'It's ten yards from the Irish goal.'

You should 'place the play' by saying something like 'Play is on the half-way line,' or 'at the sideline,' because the listeners will then think to themselves, 'I know where that is,' and it will help them to see the ball. People have to know where the action is occurring, so you must always place the play.

The commentator should not shout, or whisper. Think of

someone asking you to sing a song at a party and you start off too high, and then you get to the second verse and you think, 'Ah, Jaysus, I'm not going to be able to make the end of this.' And then you have nothing left for the finish. Commentary should be the same: you shouldn't be starting off on a 'high doh': it should be at a good, level, exciting pitch, so you can move to the other level. And then there's the level of 'the most fantastic thing ever seen.' And if it's the worst thing you've ever seen you can go down to that level.

There are games that are naturally fast—such as Gaelic football, hurling, greyhound racing, horse racing, track and field, athletics—and obviously they have to be commented on with pace. They reckon you can say three words in a second, but the 100 metres is run in ten seconds: you have time for only thirty words, so choose them well. Don't say anything superfluous, and remember to get the winner's name and the other medallists' names right.

One of the fastest games can be rugby, in my opinion, which for the most part is quite a slow, ponderous, forward game but not when it comes to the backs: then it's a case of quick hand passes and it's an up-tempo game. But at the end of this big passing movement if I am listening on the radio I want to know who scored the try, rather than the tornado of excitement from the commentator's voice. Who scored the flipping thing? That's what I want to know.

I have fantastic regard for horse racing commentators. Our own Des Scahill and Tony O'Hehir (son of the great Mícheál) are wonders, because they don't forget that the colours change in racing. Every half hour the colours change, and there are so many owners in horse racing now and so many syndicates that there are numerous colour changes. So you have to go down and check them and see what horses are in the race; and no matter how well you know them they are all over in three or four minutes and you have to go and do the next race.

People are carrying dockets in their hands and they want to know, 'Did my horse win, or where did it come in?' So make sure to get the winner right. These boys never seem to miss the winners. The boys in England, like Peter O'Sullevan, Evan Williams and the late Peter Bromley, would be high up in my estimation too but not as good as O'Hehir and Scahill, who are just unbelievable.

With regard to interviewing sport stars, in my opinion the purpose of an interview is to get information from them and not to be standing there repeating stuff you know. It sounds obvious, but there are lots of guys who do radio and television interviews who start with something twee like 'Tell me about the day you went off the road in the car. Were you in trouble with the police over that?' knowing very well they had been in jail for a month. I don't like that type of technique.

If I was giving advice to anyone about doing commentaries one of the first things I would say is to avoid clichés—not altogether but as much as possible. I heard a report recently and every cliché in the book was used, and it really takes from it. What is a cliché? A cliché is a 'time-worn phrase'—now that's a cliché too!

———

People often ask me, 'What was the biggest moment of your career, Jimmy?' I don't think there is a 'biggest' but rather a lot of big ones, like the Olympic Games every four years, which are just fantastic experiences. Every sport has its world championship, but the Olympics transcend everything, and everyone in the world has an interest in them. Doing the big world championship boxing matches is also big for me. I really enjoyed doing the 'Superstars' programmes, such as the Tour de France and World Cup and European Champions League matches.

I've done twelve Summer Olympics and twelve World Cups. I'm told by those who know these things that there are only two (both non-English speaking) people who have been at more World Cups as a broadcaster. Another big moment was doing the 1987 Tour de France when Stephen Roche won it, and doing the boxing commentary when Barry McGuigan won the featherweight world title in 1985.

I have brilliant memories. There would be a lot of favourite sporting moments, so I simply wouldn't narrow them down to just one. But one that does stick out has a connection with my father. Growing up, I used to hear them speaking about the great Jessie Owens. My father used to say, 'Ah, there'll never be another one like him.' Nobody believed that Jessie Owens, who won four gold medals in the Olympic Games in Berlin in 1936, would ever be matched. But, true enough, it ended up that I was doing commentary for the Olympics in Los Angeles in '84 when Carl Lewis exactly replicated the four gold medals of Jessie Owens. That has to be a special moment for me, as I had a flashback to sitting beside my father and listening to him talk excitedly about the great Jessie Owens.

I also have fond memories of commenting on soccer games that my son Paul, who tragically died in 2008 from motor neurone disease, played in during his career with Shamrock Rovers, Finn Harps and St Patrick's Athletic. I did three or perhaps four commentaries for television when Paul was playing, and I like to think that unless you already knew he was my son you wouldn't know this from the broadcast. But it was a bit of pressure on me, because you want him to do well and if he missed an opener you'd have to say, 'He should have hit the target.' It's not easy being critical of your own son live on air, but you can't not say it because you know him and you don't want to hurt his feelings.

I think Paul, who won a League cup title, might have had a little extra pressure in his football career from having a father who was a well-known sports commentator, but he never mentioned it to me.

———

If I'm going to be completely honest I'll also have to admit to some howlers. After all—as Joe E. Brown famously said to Jack Lemmon when he reveals he is a man masquerading as a woman at the end of *Some Like It Hot*—'Nobody's perfect.' I once famously said on air that the Argentine footballer Ardiles 'strokes the ball like it was a part of his anatomy.' And I got the boxer Jim Rock's moniker wrong by calling him the Blue Panther (instead of Pink).

But perhaps my most infamous gaffe was describing the pigeon as the symbol of peace. 'And there it is,' I memorably said during the opening ceremony of the Olympics, 'the international symbol of peace: the pigeon.' I just couldn't think of the word 'dove'.

'No, Jimmy!' the producer shouted.

And perhaps the funniest was at the opening ceremony of the Moscow Olympics in 1980 when I said, 'A beautiful piece of music specially commissioned for this opening ceremony.' As the producer then pointed out to me, 'that was nice of Beethoven to come back and write that!'

Another embarrassing moment involves a sponsored programme for Glen Abbey, a company that made men's socks and underwear. We would always have a VIP guest on the show, and essentially we would go out to the airport and get them coming in through the arrivals gate. We had the comedian Spike Milligan one time to say a few words for us.

'Spike, you're welcome to Ireland,' I told him.

'*You're* welcome to it,' he replied.

A couple of weeks later I was back out at Dublin Airport to do an interview with the legendary jazz singer Ella Fitzgerald. I decided I didn't want to get caught out again like that, so I began by saying to her, 'Ella Fitzgerald, you're welcome to the Glen Abbey Show.'

'It's sure good to meet you, Glen,' she replied.

I had a radio programme once called 'Beat the Memory Man', which went out live on either Monday or Thursday night. The formula was simple enough: there was a panel, and there would be one fellow doing horse racing, another doing music, and I was the presenter who also answered the questions. People won a guinea if they beat the panel.

I suppose my most embarrassing moment has to be on this show when a caller came through speaking in Irish, and I don't know enough Irish to conduct a conversation on the national airwaves. I knew I had to say something, as I couldn't be totally rude or ignorant, so I said, 'Agus ainm?'

'Seán . . .'

I didn't know what 'address' was in Irish, so I said, 'As Corcaigh?'

And he replied, 'Ní hea, as Luimneach.'

Then he asked a question, and I hadn't a clue what he was saying. I had to think on my feet, so I started saying, 'Hello! Seán? Seán? . . . We seem to have lost him there . . .'

And he's saying, 'No, you haven't! I'm here.'

'No, we've lost Seán. We'll try him again.' And I took him off the air, because I could think of no other way of getting out of it.

———

People always pay me the compliment of saying, 'There'll only ever be one Memory Man.' Well, I believe there's an obvious successor when it comes time for me to hang up my microphone—which, by the way, I'm not planning to do any time soon. I was driving through town during the World Cup in 2010 when the Joe Duffy show 'Liveline' rang me, and he said, 'We have a ten-year-old boy with us today who says he's deadly on World Cup facts and figures. He says one of his favourite commentators is Jimmy Magee, and we were wondering if you would be able to come on the show today.'

I explained that I couldn't make it into the studio because I had prior engagements. 'But I'd be more than happy to do a telephone call.'

The show rang me when the young fellow, named Eoin Harrington, was on air. Joe was asking him all these World Cup questions that weren't that simple for a ten-year-old, yet this young lad knew all the answers. I was really impressed. In the end Joe said, 'Jimmy, can you ask a question?'

I decided to ask him something that would give him a chance to show off his knowledge. 'What country won the World Cup and didn't lose another game for twenty-four years?'

Straight away the young fellow replied, 'That would be Uruguay. They won in 1930, and they didn't lose until the semi-final in 1954.'

I then realised that he really knew his stuff.

The show had me on again another day with Eoin, who was beginning to make a name for himself. It was arranged that I would go into the studio and they would have me on air, and then during the piece I would be brought on as a surprise guest. He was really chuffed. It turned out that he was a grandson of Liam Campbell, who was a fantastic GAA commentator and was also, as it happens, the secretary for the Jimmy Magee All-Stars from the very beginning. Liam and I were very close before he sadly passed away. I was amazed to discover that here was his grandson answering questions about the World Cup.

On the strength of his famous appearances on Joe Duffy's radio show Eoin got a couple of minor jobs with RTE, interviewing players and match reports. He reminded me a little bit of myself at that age: mind you, he's more intelligent than I was at that age and deserved the moniker 'the Memory Boy'.

Chapter 18 ∾

| SOME HARD MEN

I began the 2000s working on a show I had come up with called 'Home Thoughts from Abroad', about Irish expatriates who had played Gaelic football but ended up plying their trade in the English Premiership or with Celtic. I wanted to do it to show there are so many Irish guys whose background is in Gaelic games but who professionally ended up playing the so-called garrison game.

For example, Niall Quinn played for Dublin in the all-Ireland minor final; Kevin Moran won two all-Ireland medals; Martin O'Neill played an all-Ireland quarter-final for Derry and played in an all-Ireland colleges final; Packie Bonner played for Donegal; Kenny Cunningham played for the Dublin minors. I wanted to do pieces with them in which they were thinking of home and the Gaelic tradition. Happily, the show was a considerable success.

Earlier I wrote that the Barcelona games were the best Olympics I ever experienced, but on reflection I might have to change my mind and put it joint first with Sydney in 2000 and Beijing in 2008. Sydney was absolutely brilliant. We stayed in a hotel on the outskirts of the city, and every morning we would come in by huge double-decker trains and cross Sydney Harbour Bridge, with the Opera House just below us. What other picture postcard would you want to pick for going across to work in the morning? Sure it wasn't work at all for me.

All the little streets and avenues around the venue had the names of famous Australian Olympians: there was Herb Elliott Parade and John Landy Avenue. Typical of me, I decided to give myself more work on my time off by coming up with the idea of doing a radio programme on those streets. It was a roving-style show where I walked around the streets with my mike and told a little anecdote about each of these Australian heroes. For example, when I was in Herb Elliott Parade I would say something like 'It's a mile long, so Herb would have run it in just under four minutes, as he had famously done during such-and-such an event . . .' Then I would turn the corner into John Landy Avenue and recount something about him.

I have an uncanny gift for bumping into my sports idols when I'm abroad. Australia was no exception. I met loads of people there whom I admired, including Herb Elliott himself, who remembered me from doing the programme with him in Melbourne. 'Ah, the man from Ireland!' he said.

I also met the legendary swimmer Dawn Fraser, who was the only woman to win three 100-metre freestyle races in a row. She was a character. In 1964, at the end of the Tokyo games, in which she had won three gold medals, she was arrested for helping to pull down two Olympic flags from flagstaffs as souvenirs; but she was released and was later given one of the flags. She was banned for ten years, but the episode didn't stop her keeping her three gold medals.

———

Simply from the viewpoint of a genuine Irish football supporter I was annoyed with both Roy Keane and Mick

McCarthy for the stupid carry-on in Saipan that resulted in the team's captain—and, let's be honest, our most important player—packing his bags without even kicking a ball at the 2002 World Cup in Japan and South Korea. As far as I'm concerned they were both at fault, and they should have been big enough to shake hands and move on. Instead our chances of making an impact were dramatically reduced by Keane's decision to go home. He should never have insulted his manager with such bad language in front of the other players; but McCarthy should definitely have treated his captain a little bit better too.

In my opinion they were both wrong and they were both right. Each has to take responsibility for it. Roy was probably wrong in the way he tackled the situation about the training conditions in Saipan. He probably did it for very good reasons, but his approach and his language were wrong. And maybe McCarthy was too thick with him; you would have to say he was probably right about that also: who would put up with that?

I wasn't in Saipan when their dispute spiralled out of control and turned into something that resembled a farce—except that the only ones laughing were the other teams in our group. I still wonder how different it would have been against Spain with Keane marshalling the troops. Something tells me that the game wouldn't have ended up with us losing on penalties.

Shortly after the Saipan incident I appeared on the 'Late Late Show', and Pat Kenny asked in exasperation, 'Who's going to bring them together?' I said I would try to act as an intermediary, because I felt there was no use in everyone sitting back and doing nothing. I took it upon myself to try it, but unfortunately I got nowhere. The two of them just wouldn't come together at all. I spoke to Roy briefly, but he made it very clear that he wasn't going to budge on his decision. I tried to reason that it was so stupid that two of our main men were at loggerheads. I tried very hard and was in touch with both through their solicitors and agents and anybody else I could think of who might have been able to help sort out that terrible mess. I went through days and days of it, but the same message kept coming back to me: neither of them wanted to meet.

It was a futile exercise on my part, and I later felt that I had made an awful bloody eejit of myself by trying to bring them together. People I knew kept asking me, 'Why are you bothering when you're getting nothing yourself out of it?' But it's not the only thing I was ever a failure at!

The FAI was also blamed for the mess. It seems to me that everyone is always critical of the FAI, but I don't think it's justified. People forget that we haven't got the players: we have no Ronaldo or Silva or anyone like that, nor anyone within an ass's roar of them. Stephen Ireland won't play for us, and shouldn't be asked to either. He's not going to play now if he didn't want to play back then.

It's none of my business what sort of money John Delaney is on, but he has done well for the FAI and Irish soccer. They went out and got a manager to stem the bleeding, and Giovanni Trapattoni came in and he has certainly done that. We must remember that Denis O'Brien pays for it: the FAI couldn't even afford to pay for a top-quality manager, who is on far less than the English manager. I've only had a couple of small conversations with Trapattoni—and not about the Irish team but rather about Italy and its culture.

He has done fantastically well to get us to two play-offs and into the Euros earlier this year (2012) in Poland. But I felt the media went hysterical with his predecessors. I believe that Brian Kerr and Steve Staunton were unfairly criticised for their efforts with the Irish team. I liked Brian Kerr, a good man who tried very hard. He probably wasn't given enough time by the FAI and to my mind deserved to have his contract renewed.

After my son Paul died Kerr sent me a text he had received from Paul at a time when Paul was sick. I thought that was a lovely gesture.

It was absolutely disgraceful how the media treated Steve Staunton. I felt sorry for his poor mother, who was hounded by them in Dundalk, where she couldn't even go shopping without being taunted.

Staunton would have done much better if Bobby Robson, Lord rest his soul, hadn't become ill and been forced to step aside. We mustn't forget that the Irish team had some great results and showed potential when Robson was still there, and it only went pear-shaped afterwards when Staunton no longer had the wise shoulders to lean on.

Robson was very kind to me when he was manager of Porto. I was covering one of their matches one time and I went to the hotel to see if I could meet a few of the players who I hadn't seen before. Bobby was very accommodating. He brought me into where they were eating and introduced me to them all, which was over and above what I asked him.

———

Getting back to Roy Keane, I must say the man has been charm personified in any of my dealings with him. He has always been very friendly and has gone above and beyond the call of professional duty with me. On one occasion after a game at Old Trafford, when he was still captain at Manchester United, I was talking to him and he suddenly asked, 'Jimmy, how are you getting home?'

I told him I was on the eight o'clock flight, and immediately he said, 'You can stay with me for the night. There's no point in you running away for a flight.' It was a nice gesture from a man who apparently everybody in the game is afraid of.

On another occasion I went over to Manchester to conduct some post-game interviews with a few of the players. You had to go down to the dressing-room area and ask the official on duty for your interviewee and then he would go and see if he could get them. I went down and asked for Roy Keane.

I was told, 'Roy Keane doesn't do these interviews. Sorry.'

'Just tell him Jimmy Magee from RTE is here.'

'Oh, okay, I'll try. But don't hold your breath, mate. You'll be lucky if he comes out.'

After a few minutes he came back and he said, 'Roy Keane says you're to stay here and not make a bloody move. That's the way he said it.'

Eventually Keane came out of the dressing-room and made his way over to me and said, 'What do you want?'

'I just want a few words for the programme tonight—not a big in-depth thing.'

'Of course I will. Any time you want anything, just give me a call.'

I laughed to myself, thinking, 'This is the man they're all afraid to talk to!'

I would have nothing bad to say about Keane. You have to take people as you find them. I have seen him argumentative with other people, but not with me. It's the same with Alex Ferguson. Yes, he can be temperamental and argumentative, but he's a good person and was always good to me.

I have a nice anecdote that sums up how genuinely nice a man Roy Keane is. I walked into the canteen in RTE one evening and spotted Keane standing there talking to Steven Staunton.

When he saw me Keane said, 'C'mere! I want to have a word with you. I have a bone to pick with you!'

'What did I do?'

'You know this show of yours, "Know Your Sport", that you do.'

I was surprised he knew about it. I nodded and he continued, 'You have a guest every week on it. So how come you've never asked me?'

'Do you want to know the truth?' I said, stalling for time, because I was making this up as I went along. 'They're probably afraid to ask you; and even if you said Yes our budget is so small that we couldn't afford you.' It was near enough the truth anyway.

'I'll tell you what I'll do. You give me the okay and I'll come over. I'll pay for myself coming over. I don't want any fee, and I'll pay for my hotel. I want nothing.'

That's my Roy Keane. Lots of people are anti-Keane because of how he can be outspoken and blunt, but I have a lot of time for him as a person. As a footballer he's also up there at the top of my list of all-time great Irish players.

———

Keane wasn't the only so-called hard man to be kind to me. I did a game not so long ago at San Siro in Milan. I had booked a taxi for after the game and had it confirmed so I wouldn't be waiting around. I went to the reception area to get the taxi and waited and waited while taxis came and went without any sign of my designated lift back to the hotel. I was getting sick of looking at fellows getting into taxis. I began to realise that my taxi must have been taken by someone else. The lights began to be turned off inside the stadium. It's time to go home, and I'm still there.

I went to the receptionist, who said they had ordered the taxi for me and it had arrived. I suggested that someone else must have taken it. She told me the taxi wasn't allowed to come down to the doors, which is why I would have missed it.

By now the players were beginning to leave and I was beginning to wonder what I would do. I went up to the great Dutch player Edgar Davids, who I didn't know, as he was leaving the ground. I explained that I was stuck and asked him if there was any chance he could bring me towards Milan. 'I'm not going in that direction, but I'll leave you where you would get a taxi or a bus.' We chatted about the games as he brought me to a taxi rank in his fancy car.

———

It was a great honour being selected to do the entire commentary for the opening ceremony of the World Special Olympics in Croke Park in 2003. That was a special night, for many reasons. It was special because Nelson Mandela was there and I had the great privilege of meeting him. I also said hello that night to U2, who are probably the best Irish band of all time and one of the greatest world bands of all time—thanks to the power of the special sound that The Edge and Bono put out, and Larry's drumming alongside the bass rifts of Adam Clayton. Arnold Schwarzenegger and the Kennedys were there. It seemed that everybody was there bar Michael Jackson.

But it was also a special night because of the motorcycle parade coming into the arena, which was a joint show between the PSNI and the Garda Síochána. That must have been the first time that happened anywhere in Ireland.

I have many warm memories of the Special Olympics, but if I have to pick just one, without a doubt it involves Damien Duff, who had a fantastic World Cup in South Korea. During the Special Olympics in 2003 Irish towns were twinned with visiting countries, and the athletes stayed in those places. Some friends of mine who live in Kilcock, Co. Kildare, which had been twinned with a state in America, wanted to know if they could get Damien Duff out to say hello for an event. Nothing more. They asked if I could help arrange it. I went to Damien and he said, 'Ah, I'm no good at those things.' He's a shy and humble lad. He's also one of the kindest individuals you can possibly meet in the game. He never once became too big for his boots, even when he was one of Chelsea's stars.

'You don't have to be good at those things,' I insisted.

'Would you be there, Jimmy?'

I assured him that I would, and he said, 'You won't go away on me, will you?'

Again I reassured him that I would stand by his side throughout the event. Fair play to him, he drove out to Kilcock with Pat Devlin, and the place was jammed. I had told no-one he was coming, but the place was jammed regardless.

'Why are all these people here?' Damien asked me, surprised to see that the place was so packed.

'For you! Who else?'

'Oh, God! What am I going to say?'

'Don't worry. Just say nothing, sign a couple of autographs, and I'll get you out.'

He gave them about five pairs of signed boots, which they put up on the wall in the local clubhouse. They wouldn't let you say a bad word about Damien Duff out in Kilcock after that memorable evening.

I'm on the editorial board of the Executive Special Committee of the European Sports Journalists' Association. Every year we have a vote for the sportsperson of the year. Not surprisingly, Kelly Holmes, who won two gold medals at the 2004 Olympics in Athens, won the vote that particular year. Our president at the time was based in Stockholm, and he phoned me and said: 'The British Sports Journalists' Association have allowed us to make this presentation at their AGM, but as you are nearer to London than I am, would you go to London to make it?'

I agreed, and asked him where the statuette was. He promised he would send it by courier to me immediately. That was on the Thursday, but by the following Monday there was no sign of it. I rang him, and he assured me he had sent it. Tuesday, still nothing. The presentation was on the Wednesday.

On Wednesday morning there was still no sign of it, so I had to go to London without anything to present to her.

I had a seat allotted to me for the event right beside Kelly Holmes's seat. I had never met her before. The organisers were very reverential about people associated with royalty and the next thing I could hear was, 'Here she comes . . . Shhhh, here she comes . . . Put on your jackets.'

In comes Kelly Holmes, and the MC announces: 'Ladies and gentlemen, before our AGM we have a pleasant piece of business to do. The European Sports Journalists' Association is making a presentation to Dame Kelly Holmes, and Jimmy Magee, who is an executive member, is over from Dublin to present it.'

By now she was sitting down beside me. I stood up and said, 'Dame Kelly, I have never met you before, and I really don't know if you have a sense of humour or not, but there is only one way of finding out, if you don't mind.'

I told the story about the phone calls and how the statuette went from Stockholm to the airport in Copenhagen, that when they got it in Copenhagen they sent it back to Malmö, and then it was sent from Malmö to somewhere else . . . 'And in short I haven't got it. But if you could stand up I'll make you the presentation anyway.'

She stood up.

'Thank you, ladies and gentlemen. On behalf of UEPS I would like to present the Sportswoman of the Year: Dame Kelly Holmes.'

I held my hands up in the air as though they were holding the trophy. She could have sat down, or she could have slapped me in the face; but instead she held out her hands and took the imaginary statuette and carefully put it to one side.

'Thank you very much, Jimmy. I've got lots of awards since the Games, but this one is indeed special,' she said, and sat down again.

Some people thought it was hilarious, others thought it was cheeky. Later that day, unknown to me, Kelly Holmes had a television interview with the great Irish-born broadcaster Des Lynam. He mentioned that she had many awards and asked what the latest award was. She told him that she had received an award that day from the European Sports Journalists' Association, and asked him if he wanted to see it. She held up her two hands. He asked her who presented it to her and she replied, 'A countryman of your own, Jimmy Magee.'

'Ah, Jimmy is some man! Show it to us again.'

It was a brilliant moment. Kelly Holmes had a great sense of humour.

And I don't think she ever did get the bloody statuette.

———

Also that year I attended Euro 2004 in Portugal. I was in the stands early in the evening, long before the crowds began to swell into the stadium. Standing on the pitch was the football legend Eusébio, who played a large part in helping Portugal to reach third place in the 1966 World Cup. I had seen him play in the European Cup final in '68 against Manchester United in Wembley. And all these years later Eusébio was looking up at me and I was looking down at him. He suddenly waved in my direction, but I was thinking, 'He must be waving at somebody else, because I don't personally know him.'

I looked around but there was nobody near me. 'Wow!' I thought. He smiled, so I smiled back and then he signalled at me to go down to him. I went down and he said. 'How are you, Jimmy?'

I was flabbergasted. I had no idea how he knew my name. He must have asked someone in Portuguese television, 'Who is the man in the stands?'

We began talking about his playing days. We reminisced about how he had scored four goals against North Korea when they were already losing by three goals. He told me that he had bought a lot of property in his homeland, Mozambique, but the rebels had come along and taken it off him and he lost it all. It was a genuine heart-to-heart conversation about many different topics. It was a true pinch-yourself moment for me— one of many I've been fortunate to have experienced throughout my broadcasting career.

———

During the same tournament in 2004 I was in Lisbon—a place I love—coming from a match. All the fans were in the underground station coming back from a Portuguese match, waiting for the train. I started a song, based on the old Dean Martin song 'Volare', changing it to 'Scolari', after the Portuguese manager. I began singing on the train. 'Scolari, oh-oh-oh-oh!'

The people who were with me were asking me to stop, but eventually the whole carriage began singing 'Scolari' along with me. The whole gang of supporters on the train sang the song for the whole journey, and when they were getting out they were still singing.

———

In 2006 I decided to do a series of newspaper articles about past Olympic cities, to discover what the city was like then and what it was like now. I had no commission for this: it was just something I wanted to do for myself, knowing that I would eventually find a newspaper or magazine to publish it. I suppose you could describe it as a busman's holiday. I also thought it was an idea that had the potential to develop into a television documentary.

The first city I visited was St Louis, where the first Olympics in the United States were held. There are still parts of the place that remain from the 1904 games. Part of the old track is still there, and the old building that housed the boxing is still intact.

St Louis is easy on the eye and easy on the ear. Local people kept telling me that in a street called Blueberry Hill they have the biggest jukebox in the world. So, as a music fanatic, I had to go and see it. I couldn't believe my eyes: wall after wall and floor after floor of discs. Naturally I wanted to find the very first jukebox, and when I did I discovered that the first record on it, track A1, is 'Blueberry Hill' by Fats Domino.

As I looked at this jukebox it dawned on me that I had once been in the very bar in New Orleans where Fats Domino began his career, off Bourbon Street somewhere and below the Absinthe bar, towards St Louis Park.

After this I jetted over to Stockholm to examine the old 1912 Olympic Stadium. There's a famous story about a Japanese runner, Kanakuri Sizô, who lost consciousness half way around the marathon course because of the heat and was taken into a farmhouse to recover. He was too embarrassed to go back and run into the stadium after everyone else had finished, so he just went home. He was reported in Sweden as being missing and was searched for everywhere. In 1966 he returned, in his eighties, and ceremonially ran through the Olympic Gate to finally get his certificate for completing the race.

This was the time also when Jim Thorpe, the famous American Indian baseball player, won two gold medals but they were withheld because it was found that he had played baseball for half a dollar, or something like that, which made him ineligible. His family got the medals thirty years after his death.

I then went to Helsinki, where there are two statues outside the stadium, one to Paavo Nurmi and one to Lasse Virén. Then I went to Athens, where the original stadium still stands. My tour finished in Paris, where the games were held in 1924.

It was a fascinating tour. I really enjoyed it, and maybe some day I will get to visit all the Olympic cities. The television show is a project in hand that I think would make for great entertainment but would be perhaps too expensive to produce. You would probably want to be doing the camerawork yourself to justify making it, I suppose.

But I am actually working on a DVD with the working title *Jimmy's Olympic Files*, about all my memories associated with the games. It will be my fourth DVD: I have already done two on great sporting occasions and one on Celtic's twenty greatest moments.

————

In 2007 I was coming back from the world boxing championships in Chicago when I nearly got arrested in the airport.

I was bringing my bags through security. After years of travelling I know all too well what you can take and what you can't—and one thing you cannot take since the 'war on terror' is toothpaste. And as you probably know, the Department of Homeland Security has no sense of humour at all.

This security woman spotted the toothpaste and snapped, 'You cannot take the toothpaste with you.'

'I know that, but it's not the property of the American government. The tube of toothpaste may be but the carton is not and the toothbrush is not. Please give them back.'

'If you stop shouting I will give them to you.'

'I'm not shouting.'

After more of this nonsensical argument I said to her, 'Can I give this to you to give to George Bush and tell him to stick it.'

There was a stunned silence. She called a colleague and whispered something to him, and he in turn called the supervisor.

'Have we a problem?' the supervisor asked me.

'Actually, we have no problem at all,' I said. I began to explain the situation to him—minus my suggestion that their president, George Bush (Junior), could put my precious toothpaste in a place where the sun doesn't shine.

He said his colleagues had told him I was shouting.

'That's a lie. I wasn't shouting at them.'

He asked if I was calling them liars. I told him, 'No, I wasn't saying they were liars *per se,* I was saying that they were telling lies.'

'What's the difference?'

'Oh, there is a difference, but I don't want to get into that now,' I sighed.

He then spoke into his walkie-talkie and called down two other heavies, who came over and grabbed me by the elbows and frog-marched me off. I was brought over to a big woman in charge, whose large chest was leaning over the counter in front of her.

'What's the problem?' she asked.

I informed her that there was no problem and explained what happened. She then said, 'You said my staff are telling lies,' to which I replied, 'That's true: they are telling lies. I'm not saying they are liars, but in this case they are telling lies.'

'It's a serious accusation.'

'I'm only telling you the truth . . . Do you notice anything about me?'

She looked me up and down. 'You appear well dressed and to be a reasonable man, and gentlemanly.'

'Thank you for your kind words. But do you notice anything else?'

She thought for a second or two and then replied, 'You seem hoarse.'

'Exactly. I have had laryngitis for the last three days, which was difficult, because I am a broadcaster, and had to change my work over the last three days.'

As she seemed to sympathise with me, I asked her, 'Do you honestly think I would be able to shout, even if I wanted to?' She agreed that I couldn't. Case dismissed.

Chapter 19

ANOTHER DOUBLE TRAGEDY

The personal tragedies in my life always seem to arrive in pairs. In 1989 I mourned the death of my beloved wife and mother; and then in 2008 I was forced to endure yet another horrible year when my eldest son, Paul, and my sister Patricia were both taken from us far too early.

In 2007 my heart was shattered when Paul was told he had motor neurone disease, a horrible muscle-wasting illness. Sadly, there is no hope for this fatal illness. Life expectancy after the onset of symptoms is generally between two and five years. Approximately 40 per cent of those diagnosed live for five years, and as many as 16 per cent live another decade. While there have been rare occasions when MND sufferers have survived for more than thirty years, others have died within months of diagnosis. At best, we thought, Paul had three years; but he lasted only seventeen months.

Our relationship was more like that of brothers than father and son; perhaps this was due to the fact that we were also near each other in age—only twenty years in the difference, which is a lot when you're a child but is not so much when you're an adult. When I was fifty he was thirty, which is nothing really.

And we were quite alike. In fact he had even followed his

father into broadcasting, albeit not full-time, by doing the racing for RTE and 98FM radio for years, mostly on a Saturday. Paul was mad on horse racing; I can always remember him, even from the time he was just a little fellow, being addicted to it. He hadn't just a superficial knowledge: he had a detailed knowledge about racing, and made a fine broadcaster. In fact— and I'm not saying this only because he was my flesh and blood—I don't believe RTE used him enough: they should have had him working full-time in the Sports Department. But Paul was thrilled to be doing his Saturday broadcasts while working as public relations man for the bookmakers Boylesports.

The nightmare began when Paul rang me one day and asked me, 'Dad, do you think I'm beginning to slur my words on air?'

I told him, 'I don't think so.'

He then asked me to promise to tell him immediately if I thought he was beginning to slur his words.

Though I hadn't heard anything wrong with his voice, I sensed that Paul was very concerned, because it would be rare that he would ring me with an anxiety like that. He later told me that he first became concerned when he was on a 98FM sports show one night and one of his friends rang him afterwards and said, 'You had a fair few drinks on you tonight, Magee!'

But Paul hadn't got any drink on him. He was already beginning to worry that something was going wrong, and this remark by his friend confirmed his suspicions, as he also had pains in his arms and in his hands. He went to the GP the next day, who sent him straight away to a neurologist.

I can't begin to imagine how devastating it was for him when the results came back and the specialist told him that he had a life expectancy of three years. Paul armed himself with information, so nothing took him by surprise after that, because he knew the time limits of when things would happen.

Afterwards he met me to tell me the news. I had to fight to keep my emotions in check. I tried to make light of it by encouraging him to make the most of his time. Though clearly he was devastated, it speaks volumes for his character that he was more concerned for his young family—his son was only three at the time—and their future than for himself.

Paul adhered to my advice to live every day to the full and to fulfil some of his dreams. He had always wanted to go to Augusta for the Masters, which is without a shadow of doubt the biggest golf tournament. But it also happens to be the hardest tournament in the world to get tickets, or press accreditation, for. Before being struck down with MND Paul had frequently asked me to get him a badge for it, and when I always tried to explain that I couldn't do it he would reply, 'But you can get anything you want!'

It wasn't true, and I had tried for him, but without any success. But when he became ill a couple of people, including his very good friend Tim O'Driscoll, arranged for him to go to Augusta. Now, you simply cannot get into Augusta or play Augusta. Outsiders are out, the gates of the club are locked and there is a gate man. But somehow they arranged it all with a member of the club.

By this time Paul was in a wheelchair. He didn't realise that he was going to get inside as his friends drove their car down Washington Road to Magnolia Lane, which is the entrance to Augusta National, to meet their contact. An excited Paul couldn't believe that he was there and was asking if they thought he could get in. You can only imagine the surprise when he was told they were expecting him and they brought him up to the clubhouse.

Paul was then asked if he would like to play on the course

itself, but he replied that he couldn't play, because by this time he had lost most of the power of his arms. He was told they would get him a cart and clubs and get a caddy and go around with him. He actually played the whole eighteen holes in Augusta. With all the strength he could muster he was just able to stand to take the shot and then sit down again. He was able to swing the clubs a bit, and he got a par 3 at the sixteenth, which is a famous par 3. It's a hole that makes and breaks players at the Masters itself.

I almost played at Augusta myself, back in 1974. There was a notice on the press-room door one day (I think they do it regularly now) saying, 'Green jackets of Augusta National Course are going to give the course over to the visiting media on Monday. If interested, please add your name.'

The list was like a bridal train: it went right down to the floor, and there were so many names they had to have a draw. I was one of the lucky ones drawn to play; unfortunately I was scheduled to cover a European Cup match and I had to get back to do it, and despite my best efforts I couldn't organise a flight that would get me to Europe in time for the match. So I had to relinquish my place.

I reckon I'm the only man who ever turned down the opportunity to play Augusta; but at least poor old Paul got to play it in his dying days. After playing the course he sent me a text message: 'Dad, just had the greatest day of my life, played Augusta National.' I still have the message on the phone.

Paul's friend Tim O'Driscoll, who had helped organise his wonderful trip to Augusta, knew that Paul was a fan of Steve Staunton, who at that time was the manager of the Irish soccer team. Tim put in a call and arranged for Paul to go out to the training ground and meet all the players and get his photograph taken with the entire squad. It's a lovely picture, which I will always cherish.

My favourite photograph from this period is one taken for the magazine *VIP* of myself with my two sons, taken when we went to Dunboyne Castle. Paul was nearly banjaxed at this time, but he insisted on standing up for this picture, saying that there would never be another picture of us, and he struggled to stand up between Mark and me. We half held him up, but he insisted, 'I'm all right. I'm able to stand here on my own. Don't put your arms around me.'

It was upsetting to see Paul like this when he had been really fit—both mentally and physically—until he got that awful MND. I admired him enormously for being so determined to stand for that photograph. We just barely held him: you wouldn't notice it in the picture. He was right about it being the last picture that was taken of us together.

On another trip to the United States during his last few months Paul went over for the Superbowl. He was an American football fanatic and would drive you mad telling you everything he knew about it. He was really excited that he was going to see the Superbowl; but that was the only day in the history of the event that it rained non-stop. Of course he got soaked to the skin. He said, 'I'll get the flu or something out of this; but it makes no difference, as I'm gone anyway.'

———

As we were trying to come to terms with Paul's devastating circumstances we were dealt another blow when my sister Patricia died. Pat was the youngest in the family and was still only in her fifties when she was struck down with a brain aneurysm, which triggered a brain haemorrhage that killed her.

Up until that point she had never been sick a day in her life.

We were so close that I was almost like a father to her, as she was born a month after our father died in February 1949. It must have been hard for her to grow up without ever getting the opportunity to meet her father. She's gone now to the next world, so maybe she sees him there.

I would go regularly to Florida, where she had been living with her American husband, Michael Bagnell, and where she worked as an insurance assessor. They had no children together, but Pat had a daughter from a previous marriage.

Shortly before she died I was talking to Pat after she had just arrived back to her home in Florida from a trip to Alaska. She loved it, and was talking about getting the three of us siblings together for a holiday.

'Jimmy, you can fly in from Ireland, and Mary can fly up from New York, and we'll all go on the next trip to somewhere like the Caribbean.'

It sounded like a wonderful idea, but sadly it would never happen. She loved travel, particularly by ship. She lived in Tampa, and she would drive down to Miami to look at the cruise ships and take photographs of them. She went on a cruise at least once a year.

Shortly afterwards I got a phone call from Michael to say that she was very ill. I knew it must have been life or death from the moment I picked up the phone and heard his voice. She had got a headache and just didn't recover from it.

I booked myself on the first available flight to Florida. Emotionally exhausted from worrying non-stop on the plane, I went straight from the airport to the hospital, where I was met by my other sister, Mary, who had made her way from her home in New York.

Pat was in a coma by the time I got there, but I still talked to her, pouring out my heart as I whispered into her ear and told her how much we all loved her.

———

I don't understand this famous term 'brain-dead'. I've always thought it would be a terrible thing if you were lying in your bed and you could hear them saying, 'Will we switch it off today, or tomorrow? Sure he's gone!' And you're lying there and you can't do a thing about it. That must be something else!

From a previous experience I've always believed that people in a coma can still hear you talking to them. Many years ago I was leaving the RTE studio after doing my Sunday programme when the receptionist beckoned me over and pointed to a man sitting down who she told me had been waiting for some time in the hope of getting to talk to me.

I went over to him. He apologised for bothering me and told me that his son always listened to me on the radio and knew everything I did, because he was 'sports mad'. He went on to explain that his son, Adrian, had been in a coma for the last three months after a motorcycle accident and they were planning to switch off life support that week. He thought he could give him one last chance by me talking to his son in the hope that my voice would trigger something inside him and get him to wake up.

'For a start, you've come to the right man,' I told him. 'Under no circumstances are you to allow them to pull the plug. I'll do whatever I can.'

I went back down to the studio. Luckily, the engineer was still there, wrapping up after the programme. I explained the situation and then got the signature tune of the programme out, and I sat down and did a piece for the young man in the coma. 'Adrian, this is Jimmy Magee here. I know you've been away from us for three months, but this is what has happened since you've been away . . .' And then I explained that so-and-so had won the world snooker championship, and gave similar updates on other sports events. I did it as if it was a real news bulletin. And then I added: 'Things are very awkward, because they're going to pull the plug on your machine this coming week unless you make some effort yourself, because I know you can hear me.'

I went back down to the reception area and gave the tape to his father, who thanked me and went off.

About two weeks later the father came back again to the studio. 'He's still there, but it's all finishing tomorrow. The doctors and specialists all say he has no chance.'

I told him not to give up, and went away to do another short tape, in which I said: 'Adrian, you've had it—no chance. Isn't this terrible, and you're lying there listening to this! Try and move your little finger. Do something!'

I don't know if it was my tapes that worked, or if it was just a miracle, but Adrian woke up. More than ten years later he is now working in Dún Laoghaire as an office secretary.

—————

This inspiring story came to mind as I sat beside Pat's bedside, clutching for straws, praying for a miracle that sadly wasn't to be. Three days after slipping into a coma, which was the morning after my arrival, she passed away.

I was grateful that I had managed to get there just before she died, but it was a very difficult time. I couldn't believe what had happened, and it took a long time for me to accept that she was dead. It wasn't the natural order: I, as the eldest, should have been the one to go first.

———

Pat had left instructions that she was to be buried where she grew up, in Grange, Co. Louth. We brought her ashes back to be buried.

By this time Paul couldn't really walk, but he insisted on walking that day, with a bit of help. He was in an awful state at the funeral, because he had been close to Pat. It was probably the first time during his illness that he broke down in tears. He must have been saying to himself, 'I'm next. I can see this in all the people who are here, who will be here for me.'

He sobbed and sobbed, which wasn't like him. Perhaps I should have asked him if that's what was running through his mind—the fact that he was looking around and realising that the clock was counting down to his own funeral, and that the same faces here would be at it—but I couldn't find the courage or the words to broach such a painful subject. Instead all I could do was try to console him, to give him a hug. I couldn't even say the comforting words, 'Everything is going to be okay,' because this wasn't true for Paul.

My God, when I reflect back on it now, it was the saddest day! I'll never forget it. My sister was dead, and my son was only a few weeks away from his own death.

It was very difficult dealing with Paul's illness and, ultimately, death. He was still very young, only forty-nine, when the disease was diagnosed, which seems to be a prime age for getting it. It was sad to see how this man, strong and tough from his years getting stuck into the tackles in football and other sports, couldn't lift anything, and then suddenly he couldn't speak, which was the worst part. It broke my heart when he could no longer communicate.

I'm a regular church-goer; I'll probably attend Mass about forty-five times a year. But while I can probably be described as religious, or spiritual, I'm not a pious preacher. But if there is a Hell—and I don't believe for one moment that people burn for their sins—it will be exactly what my Paul went through in his last weeks of life. My version of Hell is the way Paul lost his voice and all movement. It was painful watching someone struggle with losing the power in their arms and fingers and then losing the power to communicate.

I don't know how he did it, but Paul did come to terms with it. He had an eternal peacefulness and a total acceptance of his destiny.

I can still remember him lying in his bed, completely paralysed and unable to open his mouth, and I said to him, 'I'd love to be able to have a conversation with you, Paul.' The only thing he could do was smile: if you told him a funny story he would smile, and he would smile for 'Yes' when I'd ask a basic question, like 'Did you get your dinner?'

He had no response for 'No'. On this particular day he was slightly grumpy, and I said, 'Oh, I wish I could do something for you! What's wrong with you? Are your knees sore?'

It was a perfectly legitimate question, because he had operations on his legs from football injuries. 'Is your back sore? Are you hungry? Did you lose all your money today on the horses?'

I was running out of ideas, and then I asked, 'Don't tell me you want your head scratched!' He beamed at me with his beguiling smile, and then I knew that he just wanted me to scratch his head—and that's not much, is it? There he was lying there and he couldn't even do that much for himself. I just couldn't begin to imagine what it was like for him not to be able to rub his head to get rid of an irritating itch.

I don't really remember my last conversation with Paul, because towards the end he couldn't speak, so it would have been a one-sided conversation. It was probably something flippant, like 'You're a bloody nuisance, wasting my time here talking to myself.' And he would smile at me—a smile that said, 'Ah, Da!' He couldn't talk, but sometimes he could just about mutter the word 'Da,' which would choke me up.

Yet despite the lack of communication he knew everything that was happening to him, because your brain is the last thing to go. Surely that is Hell, don't you think?—a capacity to know you can't do something. I've often said to people that this is my definition of Hell, while Heaven for me is peace of mind and peace of spirit. We don't often have that, do we? I don't know when I had peace of mind really—true peace of mind. Perhaps as a child I had it before my father died, but I lost it and have been forever seeking it since.

Even though we were counting the days, we were still devastated, almost inconsolable, when Paul passed away. The day he died I was doing a match in RTE and everybody posted at Paul's bedside said they would keep in touch with me. No sooner had I finished the game and the full-time whistle went than my phone rang, and it was Mark. 'You better hurry up and get here.'

I said goodbye quickly to all my colleagues and dashed out of the studio and jumped into the car and drove as fast as I could to Paul's house in Ardee. The journey was a blur; it was one of the few times that I don't even remember driving there: it must have been a record time.

'Hurry up. Paul is still alive. He's just about alive.'

I ran down the corridor, to be faced with what the nurses had told us beforehand would happen. There would be no last pain, there would be no last joke, nothing like those things that can happen in death: he would just turn on his side and die.

He was trying to hang on until I got there; when I arrived he went quickly afterwards. In the background a television was switched on, and I could hear the sound of a race commentary.

Paul watched horse racing and would have a flutter almost every day. He was so much into horses that in the late 1980s he cajoled me into getting involved in a horse syndicate. The horse was called Redundant Pal. I can't remember how much the horse cost: maybe it cost €10,000, which is substantial money now and was much more back then. We were fortunate to get Paddy Mullins, who was one of the great horse trainers, on board.

I wasn't particularly into horses, but I did enjoy the experience of going to the races with the other four in the syndicate. I didn't back very much, on the principle that if there is prize money for the race what's the point in backing your own horse if there is a chance of losing it?—whereas if there is prize money it saves you losing money. We probably did make a bit off the horse, but I personally didn't keep books.

On the day Paul died it turned out that he had backed a horse in the five o'clock, and for once his horse was doing well. When it came to the final furlong his horse was nose to nose with another horse, but Paul died before the race was over.

It was one of the most difficult moments in my life, standing at the end of my son's bed, beside his wife, Michele, watching him slip away from this world. The room was full of family members weeping. It was hard to see such a big, tough man go in such a vulnerable way.

I didn't want to cry in front of everybody, so I walked out of the room after he died, because I knew that I had to be the strong person there. I had experience of this from when my dad died. My daughters and my other son had to have someone to look up to, so I couldn't just break down.

While they all obviously missed him dreadfully, I believe I was probably sadder than anybody else apart from his wife, because we had a very close bond. I had been through the mill with Paul, particularly with going to matches and going here and there, having discussions, bringing him to England to see his heroes playing, bringing him to football and hurling matches. We did it all together.

Paul donated his brain to medical science, which I thought was a noble decision to make. At his request he was buried beside his mother, because they were very close.

The day of his funeral was horrendous for us. I was told later that it was one of the biggest funerals ever seen in Stillorgan, which was a great tribute to him. Before his death Paul told us he didn't want a lot of people saying things about him at his funeral. He said, 'If anyone is going to say anything I want it to be Dad.'

Father D'Arcy, who was the priest for his funeral, reminded me that it was Paul's wish that I would speak but added, 'It's a big thing to do, but if you feel you are up to it, do try it.'

I said, 'I'll be delighted to do it for Paul.'

With great difficulty, I got up and gave the eulogy. I told how I remembered bringing Paul home as a baby, wrapped in a blanket, on the train to Greystones, and how I thought he was the most handsome baby I had ever seen. 'This baby is now here in a box in front of us.'

He was an astonishing man, because he did everything his own way. At the funeral I told a funny anecdote about his passion for sport as a teenager. He had said to me, 'I might need your help for something.'

'What's that, Paul?'

'You know I'm running in the Leinster colleges championship on Saturday.'

'What can I do?'

'You know I'm playing football for the college in the morning first, and it's the Leinster semi-final and I have to play. So I have to get from the football to the running.'

I told him, of course, that I would bring him; but then he added that he had to get to Ballyfermot after the running, where they were playing in the under-sixteen cup semi-final in soccer.

I picked him up from the Gaelic, in which he scored two goals and five points to help his team win; then he went to the cross-country and got changed—without eating lunch or anything—and won the silver medal in the Leinster championship in a category that was four years ahead of his age; then he got back into the car and pulled off the running shoes and stuck on his football boots, and we arrived at his next destination just in time to play the other match, in which he scored four goals and his team won.

It was an astonishing performance for one man for one day, and not a bite to eat and not a word of whingeing, like 'I'm tired,' or anything.

I suppose he got his love of sport from me, but he wasn't browbeaten into it. He had come to a lot of sports events with me over the years and had seen the players, and they knew him. He was always playing with the ball, and he also took up golf and bowling; he represented Ireland in the world championships five or six times.

After Paul's death RTE planted a tree outside the Radio

Centre, half way up on the Donnybrook church side. The powers that be asked me if I would like them to do it, and they had a ceremony in his honour, which for me was both a nice and a sad occasion.

During the writing of this book I parked my car near the 'Fair City' studio, which is near the spot, and I said a little prayer for him, though I wouldn't do that regularly. It's still very painful to think about it all; instead I try to dwell on the good memories.

| MORE TRAVELS

Again I looked to work to occupy my mind after Paul's death. Happily, there was a Summer Olympics to help distract me.

I spent about five weeks in Beijing. I got off the plane jetlagged, but I thought Beijing was wonderful. They looked after us well, and we were put up in a nice hotel. We went to the Great Wall of China one day, the Forbidden City the day after, and then to the massive Tiananmen Square, which we found very poignant just thinking back to one man putting himself in front of a tank, which looked like a blip on the television screen at the time.

It wasn't a great Olympics for most of the Irish team, apart from the boxers. Countries of our size just don't have big successes at Olympic Games. Since 1924 Ireland has won twenty-three medals, with twelve of them from boxers, three of which came from the 2008 Olympic Games.

I covered all the boxing. There were five Irish boxers on the team, and each of them was beaten by the eventual gold-medallist. Kenneth Egan was very close: he was beaten by the Chinese champion, though he should have won, because of his record of having beaten the same opponent four times previously.

During the qualification group games for the 2008 World Cup a South African television station rang me, through an agent in Dublin, to request an interview with me. I wasn't too surprised, because South Africa was going to be the host country. I agreed to do it and went out to the Radisson Hotel, to be met by the television crew setting up their lights and cameras. It was a local crew—in fact I knew them all—so obviously the South African station was using a local freelance crew to keep costs down.

I was introduced to the South African presenter, and after a few minutes' chit-chat we got down to the task at hand.

As the interview began, it was quickly discovered that the sound-man's big boom microphone was picking up all the kitchen noise, and the whole crew began furiously giving out to him. They then decided that the best course was to put a mike on me. It was a complete mess. When he was putting on the mike this crazed sound-man was scratching his belly, and then he began having a running battle with the interviewer.

The interviewer apologised and in fact told me they had had too many problems with the sound-man over the previous few days. He began telling him, 'Do as you're told! You're dealing with a legend here.'

'I'll only be told that by the Ledge—right, Jimmy, right?' the sound-man replied.

He eventually got the mike on me, and we began again, when suddenly a mobile phone began to ring, and it turned out to be the sound-man's. I was flabbergasted when he actually answered it. 'No, I'm at work. No, I'm workin'! I'll see yeh tonight . . . I'm with Jimmy Magee here—yeah, the legend.'

After a bit more of this nonsense the comedian Jason Byrne came out and revealed that the sound-man was the one and only Brendan O'Carroll in disguise, and that the whole episode had been organised for the popular television show 'Anonymous'.

I think they were a bit disappointed that I wasn't fuming. When I see it now I think it was bloody funny. All I did throughout the ordeal was simply sigh—but I did ask at one point who was in charge, and said we'd never get it done.

I never twigged it was Brendan, even though I knew him quite well. He even asked me to appear in his film *Sparrow's Trap*, which sadly never saw the light of day, because of funding problems half way through filming.

My day's filming was another hilarious event. When I arrived on set I was handed the script and was disappointed to discover that they wanted me to use the 'f' word on camera. When I refused, Gerry Browne, the film's producer and one of its co-stars, said to me, 'But it's in the script.'

'I know that.'

'Then just say it.'

'No. I won't use bad language.'

Years later Gerry Browne confessed to one of my colleagues, 'Do you know what? Jimmy was dead right not to use that word, even though it was in the script.'

———

Unfortunately, Ireland didn't get to South Africa in 2010, because of the infamous double-handball episode by Thierry Henry during the soccer play-off with France in Paris. I was disappointed not only for the Irish team, who—let's be fair— played France off the pitch that night, but with the bad example in sportsmanship Henry sent out to the youngsters watching that night. He was essentially saying, 'It's acceptable to cheat.' No, it's not.

He maintains that he didn't cheat by controlling the ball with his hand—not once but twice—but I can't find any other word to describe his action, which led to France scoring the winner. But who is to say that Ireland would have won on penalties? Maybe we would have got to South Africa, maybe we wouldn't. But France went over and made a holy show of themselves with their internal bickering, and couldn't even get out of their group. Perhaps it was bad karma.

I remember the South African World Cup for the wonderful football, particularly by Spain, the deserved winners. It's rare that the team that is the most attractive on the eye wins these tournaments.

I also did a few little side trips. I had been there twice before, and I knew where to go and see things I hadn't seen before. Sadly, South Africa was one of the few places that Marie didn't get to go with me.

I enjoyed being in the thick of the action and soaking up the fabulous carnival-like atmosphere at that World Cup. I know many people had been talking before the tournament about the corruption and the worrying amount of crime in South Africa, but I have nothing but good memories of my time in Cape Town, which is just a gorgeous place and one of the world's nicest places, with friendly—and honest—people, as I discovered one day.

I wanted to eat in this particular place and I hadn't got any South African money: I only had a couple of hundred euros. I couldn't find anywhere to change it, so this waiter said she would get it changed, as there was a bureau de change up the street. I gave her €200, and off she went. She arrived back shortly later with the South African equivalent. Now, there are not a lot of places where you could do this and the person would come back.

There was one fantastic day in March 2009 that will forever live on in my memory. It started with Ireland winning the Grand Slam in Rugby and ended that night with Bernard Dunne's world title fight.

In rugby, Ireland had previously only won one Grand Slam, in 1948, until that fateful day in 2009 when Brian O'Driscoll led them out to win it again. Later I sat at a dinner with Brendan Bowyer—a man who has seen all the rugby greats—when he was getting the freedom of Waterford. He said that night that Brian O'Driscoll is 'morally, physically, mentally' the toughest man on a rugby pitch, that nothing fazes him. I agree with him; but if you had to pick Ireland's greatest sportsperson then you'd also have to put Seán Kelly and Stephen Roche into the mix for consideration.

———

After the Grand Slam victory that night I headed down to the O2 Arena at the North Wall to do the commentary on the Dunne fight. I've been up close to Bernard throughout his career, so being there that night watching him win was very special for me.

It was the night also when the woman boxer Katie Taylor got into the ring before the fight. As I said on commentary that night, she is the most spoken-about Irishwoman: everybody was talking about her, but nobody had ever seen her, and here she was on what turned out to be a momentous day in Irish sports history, in front of this big audience on live television. Whatever reputation she had before she now had a 'live' reputation, and people now knew who she was and how talented she really was. Last year (2011) Katie won the European title again—five in a row, and four world titles in a row. She is just unbeatable. In my opinion she is Ireland's greatest contemporary sportsperson.

———

Last year I was travelling through Castlebar when a boxing promoter named Michael Hennessy left a voice message on my mobile phone: 'Jimmy, will you call me? It's a matter of urgency.'

I returned the call. He asked me if I was interested in doing commentary in Britain. I said, 'The answer is yes; however, I'm tied into a contract . . . but tell me more.'

He said he was going to get Mark Sharman, who used to be head of Channel 4 and was now putting together a boxing package for Channel 5, to give me a call with the details.

When Mark eventually phoned me he said, 'You're the man I want for this. There's no major terrestrial boxing in England any more, but Channel 5 is doing it, and the first big fight is Tyson Fury and Chisora.'

I told him I couldn't do it, because it was such short notice. He then admitted that they thought they would have someone else but couldn't get them, and he was told, 'There's only man to get, and that's Jimmy Magee.'

'Anyway,' I told him, 'I'll think about it.' And I did. In fairness to them I must say that a few people in RTE said to me, 'Go for it,' but unfortunately the right person didn't tell me to go for it, and I wasn't going to have a situation similar to what occurred over my deal with UTV. After all, RTE is my bread and butter. So

I had to say, 'Thank you for thinking of me, but I can't do it.'

The fight itself was a huge success, as was the terrestrial boxing coverage. They have now signed a new contract to do it more regularly; so I missed out badly on that one. I didn't do it because I believe that the umbilical cord is still attached to RTE, that in my head I think I still owe them something.

————

I also worked for Croatian television at the World Cup of Athletics in 2010. They have an English-language service, and they asked me to do the commentary for them, which was a brilliant experience.

I'm on the Executive Board of the European Sports Journalists' Association, and I was appointed in 2011 to AIIPS, which is the world body, and to its new Ethics Commission for Sports Journalism. On it there is a Swiss solicitor, an Austrian professional and myself. I am the president of the World Sports Ethics Commission.

What is ethics? Staying away from brown envelopes!

I have to travel quite a bit in these roles, and in November that year I was invited to Baku, the capital of Azerbaijan, for countless official dinners. There was toast after toast: it seemed that after every mouthful there was a toast. This guy was explaining to me about the toasts. 'When you stand up to say a toast you have to say something that applies to the time we are in or to somebody at the table. It has to be relevant.'

Eventually I had to make a toast. I began with 'I am very pleased to be making a toast. I come from Ireland, and as you are holding the Eurovision Song Contest next year I am more entitled to speak of the Eurovision than anyone else, because

Ireland has won it more times than anyone else.'

'Johnny Logan!' they all began shouting. I thought it was amazing to discover he was a household name in that part of the world. I told them that I knew Johnny Logan, because he had played football with the All-Stars. For the record, he was a good player.

I get great enjoyment out of the success and the admiration that these Irish stars receive around the world. I was once in Madison Square Garden in New York at a function, and the announcer said that that they had the 'chairman of the boards' with them tonight. Who's that? you're probably wondering. There's only one chairman of the boards: Eamonn Coghlan. At the mere mention of his moniker every person stood up in the stadium and gave him a standing ovation. I was impressed that an Irishman who had long since retired, and wasn't one of their own, was so warmly received.

EPILOGUE

I've done a lot of firsts in my time. I covered the first indoor world track and field championships. Funnily enough, I was at the 1977 Grand National when Red Rum became the first and only horse to win it for the third time. I was covering the match when Ajax won the Champions League (called the European Cup back then) for the third consecutive time in 1973, and in 1976 when Bayern Munich did likewise.

With regard to covering the FA cup final, unfortunately I can't claim to be the first but I can lay claim to being the second broadcaster to cover an FA cup final for RTE. I covered the 1967 final between Chelsea and Spurs, which had its own 'first': it was, surprisingly, the first time the FA cup final had been contested by two teams from London, which is a hard one to believe.

What was the greatest moment of my career? I don't think there is a greatest: there are a lot of big ones. Every four years there's the Olympic Games, which are just fantastic. Every sport has its world championship, but the Olympics transcend everything, and almost everyone in the world has an interest in them. Doing the world championship boxing matches is also special for me. I really enjoyed doing the Superstars programme, the Tour de France, the World Cups. It's hard to single out any event. I've enjoyed it all, every single moment.

While putting this book together I was preparing to go over to the Olympics in London. At the beginning of the 2000s I declared that my ambition was to see one more Olympic Games. Sure I've seen three more since then—2004, 2008 and 2012—and hopefully I'll make it through another decade of Olympics. At the moment I'm able to work and am not affected by anything.

I'm seventy-seven, going on fifty-seven! I haven't changed really in the last twenty years. Thankfully, I'm still healthy and full of zest to continue working. What keeps me going is the future. What am I going to be doing in the future? Where am I going to be? To be in London this year (2012), to be in Brazil in 2014 for the World Cup, and to be in Rio in 2016 for the next Olympic Games after London. I intend to keep going until I'm not able to work any more. I want to work until my last breath—although I don't want to die like that, necessarily: I'd prefer a bit of time lying in bed so I can prepare properly to meet St Peter at the Pearly Gates. Hopefully there'll be a sports broadcasting station in Heaven that will be hiring when it's my time to go there.

Sometimes I hear myself on shows, such as 'Reeling In the Years', and I'm amazed to hear that my voice hasn't changed at all during the intervening years; it hasn't got tenors and baritones, as you might expect. So why stop, unless you're annoying people or somebody doesn't like you any more?

It quite annoys me when people dictate whether or not you are able to do something because of your age. It also annoys me when people say something along the lines of 'God, he's very young to be playing in a big match like that. He's only eighteen!' Or 'Your man's too old at thirty-eight to be still playing, isn't he?'

But can he play? Well, if he can play under pressure he's good enough. I don't care what age they are, as long as they can play.

It annoys me to think that people might start tagging me in

a similar fashion, because I'm firmly convinced that if you're able to do something you're able to do it, irrespective of what age you are.

Of course the natural order of things is that people are at their best maybe between their mid-twenties and mid-thirties, and I wouldn't argue with that. For me there are six senses: all the five senses that everyone else has, and then there's the sixth sense, called common sense. What I mean is, if you're able to do it you should continue doing it until you're not able to do it any more. I think you'll know yourself when your time has come—when you've mislaid stuff or made a couple of mistakes, even if nobody else notices them. It's time then to take a long, hard look in the mirror.

Look at our fabulous president, Michael D. Higgins. He was the oldest candidate in the presidential election in 2011, but he was clearly also the best person for the job, getting an unprecedented million votes. Not bad for someone in his seventies!

Before that election I was flabbergasted to be approached and asked if I'd consider running for the presidency. Two particular influential groups asked me if I would be interested in going for it. It had never entered my head. Sure why would it? The presidency! What right would I have? I'd have no right to do something like that. I laughed, in fact, when I was asked.

Shortly after that I was at an event in Castlebar when the Taoiseach, Enda Kenny, came over and sat down beside me, and we began to chat. He said to me, 'There's a rumour going around that you've been asked to run for the presidency.'

I admitted that that was indeed true, and he told me, 'You'd do well.'

Perhaps he was only saying that to be nice to me, but it got me thinking all the same, and I sounded out a few close friends and family members.

A good friend very wisely asked me, 'Would you like all your private life to be open to scrutiny?' This was long before the publicity of the campaign kicked off and turned the election into one of the most vicious ever, with personal attacks and probing into the candidates' lives. 'No, I wouldn't fancy that— even though I've nothing to hide,' I replied.

'Forget about running for president so!'

That was good advice, and I took it. I thanked God I didn't enter the race when I saw all those people being knocked: Mary Davis because she was on a few boards; Dana because of her brother; David Norris because of his outspoken views and that infamous clemency letter for his former lover; and Seán Gallagher for his connections with Fianna Fáil.

I'm planning to take one last major sojourn, which I'm describing in my head—as I used to do all those years ago when I did pretend commentary as a young boy—as the Jimmy Magee Farewell Tour, for want of a more original title.

You might be asking yourself now, A farewell to what? I want to revisit where I have enjoyed in my life, to go back to some of the events I have loved, to go to some of the places that I always wanted to go to and never did. It will take at least four years, and it will culminate in the Olympic Games in Rio de Janeiro in 2016. I'll be eighty-one years old by then, but knowing me I'll probably have thought of some other mad scheme to do to keep me going.

Last year I was listening to a man called John McCarthy from Cork on the radio talking about his battle with motor neurone disease, which took my son. He was very interesting and funny as he talked about the things he still wanted to do. Though he was very positive and hands-on in everything he does, that is one thing I don't want to happen to me—anything but that, please God.

Without wanting to sound morbid, I've already thought about how I would like my funeral to be. I'd like to have a Dixieland jazz band playing at the cemetery, and then I would like a really good George Jones country song, sung by Ray Lynam, with its poignant lyrics, 'He Stopped Loving Her Today'.

And then to finish the musical party for my funeral I'm going to have tenors singing, so nobody could say I didn't give them variety.

INDEX